WHY PREACH

Encountering Christ in God's Word

PETER JOHN CAMERON, O.P.

WHY PREACH

Encountering Christ in God's Word

IGNATIUS PRESS   SAN FRANCISCO

Nihil obstat: Rev. Msgr. J. Warren Holleran, S.T.D.
Imprimatur: † Most Reverend George Niederauer
Archbishop of San Francisco
January 9, 2009

Front cover photograph:
Crowds in Saint Peter's Square
© David Lee / Corbis

Cover design by Roxanne Mei Lum

© 2009 by Ignatius Press, San Francisco
All rights reserved
ISBN 978-1-58617-272-5
Library of Congress Control Number 2008933493
Printed in the United States of America ∞

FOR
ROMANUS CESSARIO, O.P.

CONTENTS

PREFACE

This book is intended for priests (and those preparing to be ordained priests), whose first duty, the Church tells us, is to preach: "Bishops, with priests as co-workers, have as their first task 'to preach the Gospel of God to all men,' in keeping with the Lord's command" (*Catechism of the Catholic Church*, no. 888, quoting *Presbyterorum Ordinis*, no. 4). A particular provocation for the book is Pope Benedict XVI's direct statement in *Sacramentum Caritatis*: "Given the importance of the Word of God, the quality of homilies needs to be improved" (no. 46). *Why Preach* hopes to help with that improvement.

The book stems from my priesthood, my own preaching, and from my experience of teaching homiletics (beginning in 1994) at Saint Joseph's Seminary, Dunwoodie; the Pontifical North American College, Rome; the Dominican House of Studies, Washington, D.C.; and elsewhere.

This is not a how-to book on preaching. Rather, the objective of the book is to persuade preachers to think about preaching in a new way. Its aim is to provide a fresh and, I hope, helpful re-conception of preaching geared to deepening a preacher's appreciation of what preaching is so as to increase his desire to preach.

I realize that some priests find preaching intimidating, tedious, or even futile. It's a grind to put the regular weekly effort into preparing a homily when the fruits of preaching seem so meager: people do not pay attention, they are critical, or they do not offer any response at all. We can easily become dismayed over preaching that appears ineffectual, that seems not to reach anyone. My earnest hope is to address all that and offer a way out.

You will see that I have drawn heavily on the writings of Pope Benedict XVI, including the many works that predate his elevation to the See of Peter.

The first word of thanks is due to my fellow friars of the Order of Preachers who taught me what Holy Preaching is, why it is crucial, and what it means to do it well. With special affection, I would like to thank my Dominican theology professors, in particular Father Romanus Cessario, O.P., my first teacher and friend. I am deeply grateful to Father Francis Martin, my mentor in the study of Sacred Scripture. I thank also Father Peter Girard, O.P., the Director of Continuing Formation for the Province of Saint Joseph who expedited my sabbatical, and Father Dominic Izzo, O.P., Prior Provincial.

Also, I owe an untellable debt of gratitude to the ecclesial movement Communion and Liberation. A major portion of what is contained in this book comes from what I have learned from the writings of the late Monsignor Luigi Giussani, the saintly founder of Communion and Liberation, from the priests and laypeople who follow its charism, from those who educate others about it, and from my friends in that movement, especially Father Rich Veras.

In a special way, I am deeply thankful to the Dominican friars of Saint Dominic's Priory in Youngstown, Ohio: Father Regis Heuschkel, O.P., Father William Rock, O.P., Brother Thomas Aquinas Dolan, O.P., Father Giles Dimock, O.P., Father Jordan Turano, O.P., Father Rick Jastrzebski, O.P., along with their prior and my friend Father James M. Sullivan, O.P. It was Father Sullivan's idea for me to take a short sabbatical at Saint Dominic's Priory in order to write this book, and for that insight along with all his goodness and generosity to me I am deeply grateful. These friars generated me by their fraternity, hospitality, encouragement, example, instruction, correction, community, and prayer. I could not have written this book without them.

Thanks also to the people of Saint Dominic's parish, Youngstown, Ohio, to the Dominican brothers and guests visiting the priory during my stay there, to Jeanne Shanahan for her clerical assistance, and in a special way to Catherine Kolpak, my assistant at *Magnificat*, who helped me prepare the manuscript for publication—a woman who seems to know how to make miracles happen.

—*Peter John Cameron, O.P.*
Solemnity of Saints Peter and Paul
June 29, 2007

Why Preaching

"How necessary is the office of preaching without which the human heart would not rise to the hope of heaven."

—Bl. Humbert of Romans, O.P.
A Treatise on Preaching, 13th century

ONE LABOR DAY NOT LONG AGO, a close member of my family suffered a devastating medical trauma. When the call came, my family and I—spread throughout the Northeast—immediately jumped in our cars in Massachusetts, Rhode Island, New York, and Connecticut and raced to the hospital in Hartford. We hurried to the emergency room waiting area, and there we did all that we could do: we waited. And worried. And waited. From what little we knew, the situation was dire. The passing of each mute and interminable minute made things seem more ominous. We sat with our eyes glued to the door, dying for a doctor to come through it to report that the one we loved was not going to die. Our whole life, in anguished anticipation, was fixed on that announcement; our entire existence had become one huge begging for a life-giving word. We were not going to leave that place without it. And then it happened. The door opened. The physician appeared. And the announcement was made: The condition was serious—very serious. But ... he would live. The news was good.

I would venture to say that many people live their lives in more or less the same predicament. Almost every day of their lives they confront some crisis ... maybe a calamity ... at the very least some conflict (even though they may not be aware of it). And in the face of it, they feel utterly powerless. They will not give up, but they know that, on their own, they cannot conquer or quell the problem that oppresses them. They live waiting for a Word that will make a difference ... for breakthrough News. They will not leave without it. And the only thing that can give them relief, that will enable them to go on, is the arrival of an expected authority, who at long last appears, who comes specifically for them, mindful of their agony, and who proclaims to them Good News.

This is why there is preaching in the Church.

How our hearts rose up with the hope of heaven when the doctor spoke those astonishing words to us in the waiting room. With them, we could begin again. And it was not simply because we were given encouraging "information". Those words contained and communicated a *reason*. They quickened in us a strength, a resiliency, a resolve we never knew we had. We could go on. The doctor's words were a birth for us. Exquisitely true is the promise we read in the Letter of James: "Of his own will he [the Father] brought us forth by the word of truth.... Receive with meekness the implanted word, which is able to save your souls" (Jas 1: 18, 21). God's people are dying for this Word.

In the eloquent expression of the Letter to the Hebrews, "the Word of God is living and active, sharper than any two-edged sword, piercing to the division of soul and spirit, of joints and marrow, and discerning the thoughts and intentions of the heart" (Heb 4:12). The living and effective razor of God's Word confided to the preacher penetrates our impenetrability (the root of all immorality), pierces the nihilism that suffocates us like a shroud, and slices through our debilitating sorrow, severing whatever ensnares us in desolation. By his faithful preaching of the Gospel, the preacher reveals people's hearts to themselves, gives them the power to make judgments that liberate them, and imbues them with the certainty, confidence, and gladness before which hell itself cowers.

This is why there is preaching in the Church.

But preaching is not speech-giving. No one was ever saved by a message. It would have been a waste of time for the Word to become flesh if it sufficed for the Father to send a memo instead of his Son. No one was ever saved by a mere discourse. Preaching is so much more than this. The history of civilization is rife with ingenious, mesmerizing, virtuous prophets, visionaries, and teachers. And yet, people today remain as confused, miserable, prone to malice, cynical, negative, fearful, lonely, and lost as they ever were. Something more than a good teacher is required. According to Joseph Cardinal Ratzinger (now Pope Benedict XVI), the aim of preaching "is to tell man who he is and what he must do to be himself. Its intention is to disclose to him the truth about himself, that is, what he can base his life on and what he can die for." [1] And that disclosure is not a discourse; it is an *encounter*.

For people in pain, a preacher has the chance to make a drastic difference. Diffidence, doubt, and despair congregate in the ordinary person's life to the point of overcrowding.

---

[1] Joseph Cardinal Ratzinger, *The Nature and Mission of Theology*, trans. Adrian Walker (San Francisco: Ignatius Press, 1995), pp. 62, 63.

The only antidote is the Presence of Someone else there. Someone whose winning attraction can dispel the prevailing darkness and completely captivate the heart.

After the Ascension of Jesus Christ, the people were spellbound at the preaching of Saint Peter (who was transformed by the grace of Jesus Christ). In response to Peter's preaching, the people begged, "What shall we do?" (Acts 2:37). In Peter the preacher, they had found an authority in whom they were eager to entrust their pitiful lives. Perhaps for the first time, the people saw that it was possible for them to change ... that they could live in a transformed, meaningful way ... that hope was a reasonable strategy. As moving as Peter's words were, something more than a sermon won them over that day, namely, Peter's presence. That is why on sunny days the people would carry their sick into the streets and lay them on mattresses arranged on the road—so that Peter's shadow might fall on them (Acts 5:15). The people recognized the power even of Peter's *darkness*—his shadow—to overcome *their* darkness.

This is why there is preaching in the Church.

CHAPTER I

The Starting Point of Preaching:

Beginning from Human Experience

"We had the experience but missed the meaning, and approach to the meaning restores the experience."

— T. S. ELIOT

WHY DO SO MANY PEOPLE find preaching so boring? Because it fails to begin from their *experience*. Don't mistake the term "experience" for something subjective. Just the opposite. "Experience" best understood refers to what is most universal, what is most commonly shared and innate to every human being. Experience is our basic, our original, condition. It is the criterion that has been put in our hearts for acknowledging the truth.

Think about an occasion when someone desired to speak to you. Why did you agree to listen? We listen when we expect to hear something that will be relevant to our lives, something pertinent, interesting, perhaps even important for us. We give way to what the speaker has to say if we are convinced that the question "What's in it for me?" will somehow be answered. Notice how we refer to letters, e-mail, and written communication in general as "correspondence"—an intriguing expression. Correspondence is what we are looking for when we consent to listen to another. Correspondence with what? With that which is most urgent, vital, essential for our lives. We are willing to listen to another once we have the assurance that the words spoken will address our *experience*, that is, our constitutive need for truth, beauty, love, goodness, justice, and happiness.

The Starting Point of Experience

To get at this sense of "experience", consider a mundane example: choosing a movie to go see. In the decision-making process, we ask: What's the movie about? Who's in it? Who directed it? How was it reviewed? What are the performance times, the ticket price, the cinema? etc. In trying to decide whether or not to go see a particular movie, we compare the various values of the movie with our intrinsic, indelible needs: our need for truth, beauty, love, goodness, justice, and happiness. If the subject matter of the movie seems suitable and worthy, it corresponds with our need for truth. If we like the actors, director, and cinematographer, then the movie corresponds with our need for beauty. If reliable critics have endorsed the film, we may be better assured that our need for goodness will be met. A reasonable ticket price, show time, and location contribute to our need for justice. And the ultimate sense that somehow seeing the movie will enrich or delight us is what corresponds to our need for happiness. We go to the movies for various reasons—for entertainment, to be educated, edified, to escape—and yet what moves us to go to *this* movie at *this* moment is that we have compared the value of the movie with all those needs of our hearts—our elementary experience—and made the judgment that the experience of going to see the film will do us some good.

Judgment, based on experience, then, is that faculty we are born with that equips us to face reality in order to make the best sense of it. I start from experience when I use my intellect to compare whatever is before me with the natural criteria in my heart so as to make a fitting judgment that becomes conducive to my personal fulfillment. This understanding of elementary or original experience is at the heart of the description of the human heart in the *Catechism of the Catholic Church (CCC)*: "The heart is the dwelling-place where I am, where I live.... The heart is our hidden center, beyond the grasp of our reason and of others.... The heart is the place of decision, deeper than our psychic drives. It is the place of truth, where we choose life or death. It is the place of encounter" (no. 2563). The trouble is that the common mentality, in talking about the heart, tends to reduce it to something sentimental or "romantic"; thus, the term *heart* can be misleading or unhelpful for some. But just as we are able to appreciate the delicious taste of some food because of our sense of taste; just as we are able to delight in a beautiful sight because of our sense of sight or to participate in a hearing because of our sense of hearing, so too are we able to make sense of experiences in our life because of our "sense" of experience—our elementary or original experience.

A key sign of adult maturity in a person is the accustomed habit of comparing everything in daily life with elementary experience (as opposed to approaching everything from the compromise of "the common mentality"). If we neglect or resist this, then our original needs come across as foreign to us. Life becomes oppressive, as if a hard crust has formed over it.

The more a preacher is aware of this fundamental exigency of experience, and the more he deliberately makes reference to it and allows it to form his conception of preaching, the better chance he then has of reaching his hearers, for this integral need for truth, beauty, love, goodness, justice, and happiness continues to weigh on us; in the words of Saint Augustine, our hearts are restless. And experience is the means by which people search for truth and meaning in their lives. The fact that I detect in myself the insistence of this relentless need only further proves how much I require truth and meaning in my life ... meaning that I cannot find in myself. In our ongoing search for meaning, we eagerly compare whatever we come across with these fundamental criteria of our hearts intent on finding a correspondence that will bring our search to a jubilant end.

Experience, then, must be the starting point for preaching if it is to be effective. That is to say, the preacher must be aware of his own profound need for truth, beauty, love, goodness, justice, and happiness, and he must be attentive to this condition in his hearers. Recognizing and respecting this fact about the human heart is imperative for preaching. Any *answer* that a preacher intends to offer his people must be in response to a *question*. Giving the answer to a question that has never been asked is the perfect definition of boring. The answer might be brilliant, ... but if I do not comprehend its relevance to my life, if I cannot grasp how it corresponds to what is urgent and important to me, then it is not worth listening to.

Like nothing else, attentiveness to our original experience provokes in us certain unavoidable and crucial questions: How did life come to be? What is the meaning of life? Why is life worth living? Is there a purpose and a design to it all? Does faith or religion make any difference? What is the key to happiness? To ignore or dismiss these questions would make us less human. Any such refusal would impede us from becoming fully ourselves, for our meaning is caught up in these questions. Even more, our experience reveals to us that to be human is *to be* a question. At the same time, experience makes it clear that the Answer we require is not inside us. We are always looking for something more. We constantly are searching for Something within something. If we cannot come to terms with the ultimate reasonableness of reality, then existence actually seems threatening to us, reality seems menacing.

What the Preacher Is Up Against

Tragically, many people live separated and distanced from their elementary experience. They subsist without an awareness, a sensitivity to the original design and demands of their hearts. And without that awareness, if they venture to explore life in order to make sense of it, the only thing left for them with which to begin is an abstraction. If a person lives divorced from his own heart as the criterion for all fulfillment, then that person gives up the search for what *corresponds* with that heart. To that extent, he forfeits the chance for real happiness.

Pope John Paul II, the great champion of the New Evangelization, once stated (at a meeting in Rimini, Italy, in 1982) that the basic human drama is the failure to perceive the meaning of life, to live without a meaning. This is what happens when people lose touch with their elementary experience, with the original needs of their own hearts. Yet that loss of perception began to infect mankind the moment that Adam and Eve committed their sin.

We live without a meaning because we live enmeshed in the effects of original sin. Original sin distorts our reason so that we contrive to contort reality to conform to our own ideas, our whims, our will. The sabotage of original sin dupes us into measuring reality according to some pre-fabricated standard of our own concoction. That is, we minimalize the ultimate meaning of things to something that we can comprehend, manage, dictate, and manipulate. We want to remake things according to our own measure. Original sin attempts to identify the total value of everything with something that we can conceive of and understand—to base reality on some aspect of our own selves. If someone succeeds in re-creating "god" according to his own image and ideas, then reality gets reduced to an idolatry over which he presides as the sole, indomitable deity.

At the same time, the more we strive to explain everything by way of an idol, the more miserable we become, because an idol simply can never be enough for us. Never. An idol is not the Something within something that the infallible heart craves. The tyranny of original sin may be strong, but the desires of the heart are stronger. The heart knows infallibly what corresponds to its longing; it knows infallibly whether or not something satisfies it.

This dilemma of original sin constitutes one of the most formidable obstacles that a preacher will ever have to face. For how do you preach about God to people who have decided to depose him and put themselves in his place? No god is useful if usurped. Thus, the preacher contends with an impossible impasse. Those under the spell of original sin (namely, ourselves) are the ones who need to hear the Good News more than anyone else, yet they are the first to dismiss preaching as insipid, futile, even fatuous. All the same . . .

It is the preacher's vocation to give people back their hearts.

If a preacher has an appreciation of elementary experience—of the genius of the human heart—then he stands a chance of freeing his hearers from original sin's idolatrous individualism. How? By reintroducing people to what is more original to them than original sin, namely, their "I".

The "I"

A vital device for converting those caught up in the debilitation of original sin is reminding people of the salient facts proper to their humanity—their own "I". These are truths readily evident to anyone who takes the time to reflect on his own self and to acknowledge what is essential about it. But to the extent that we neglect to live with such self-examined awareness, we blithely become detached from our I, we lose a sense of our true self, and we capitulate to a deficient way of approaching reality.

What do I mean by this? Again, we must begin by looking at our own experience. Simple self-reflection brings up certain incontestable facts—all of which raise Big Questions for me and my I.

I Am Made

To start with, I'm here. Where did I come from—because one thing I am certain of is that I am not responsible for bringing about myself; I did not create my I; my existence is not of my doing. Even more, I cannot make myself to be the way I think I might like to be. There are very concrete things about myself that, left to myself, I simply cannot change. So it is fair to ask: Who did make me? And I purposefully ask *Who* and not *What*, because my Maker—however we conceive of our Maker—must be at least as

advanced as I am, and I am not a radish or a trilobite; I am
a person—I am a *who*.

That said, a fundamental, irrefutable fact about my existence is that I am in relationship to the One who made me.
To be human is *to be* a relationship with our Maker—to be
human is *to be* a relationship with the Infinite. For what is
finite—me—can be brought into being only by Another
who is Infinite.

Which leads me to wonder, *Why* do I exist? I didn't have
to be. Someone decided to put me in the world. To be an
I is to be part of a belonging. And since I in no way earned
or merited that accomplishment, I am left to conclude that
my creation was an act of sheer *mercy*. Someone, on his own
initiative and for his own reasons, decided that it was good
for me to exist.

And I do mean good. Our own experience confirms that
we make what we like. If it is time to make dinner, and
your choices are the delicious lasagna your grandmother
used to make or that brussels-sprouts-lima-bean-parsley-
and-liverwurst casserole you hated as a kid, what's it going
to be? You end up making what you like. Which implies
that if I am made, then my Maker likes me ... maybe even
loves me. Because in the depths of my heart—as I examine my elementary experience—I am convinced that I am
not here to be a slave. I am meant to be free; freedom is
my destiny. All of this indicates that my existence has a purpose. If I *am*, then I can conclude that I *have* a meaning, a
mission. And to be fulfilled, I need to know what that mission is. But I cannot find it in myself. In order to understand some strange object that we have never seen before,
we ask its maker to explain what it is. So too, in order to
understand myself, I have to appeal to my Maker. My *I*
cries out to the *You* who made me, begging for that answer.

I Am Infinite

Don't get scared. If to be human is to be in a relationship with the Infinite, as discussed above, then our confidence in that reality increases as we consider another undeniable truth about the *I*: There is something about me that is infinite. And what is that? My *desires*. My desires are boundless. I possess an infinite desire for truth, for affection, for understanding, for beauty, for delight, for companionship, for peace, for contentment, for acceptance. We are never satisfied with what we have. Everything in us clamors for something *more*. We are plagued by a kind of inherent dissatisfaction. At the heart of the self is a longing, a desire, a thirst, a need that pushes us throughout life to grab onto any candidate likely to answer those indefatigable desires.

Yet, being finite, I cannot fulfill my infinite desires. And this often leads to undesirable frustration. For neither can I suppress nor amputate my desires. They persist in working on me no matter what I do. So much is this the case that I realize that to be human is *to be* desire. *I am* unsatisfied longing. And just as I did not give myself my existence, I realize that I did not give myself my desires. My desires are *given*. Recognition of the fact that I cannot satisfy them leads me to surmise that my desires are given to me precisely to lead me to the One who gave them to me in the first place.

In the words of C. S. Lewis, desire "has [always] summoned you out of yourself. . . . The thing you long for summons you away from the self." [1] If there is some*thing* infinite about me, then it only stands to reason that there must be some *One* who is infinite. Father Rich Veras once

[1] C. S. Lewis, *The Problem of Pain* (San Francisco: HarperCollins, 1996), pp. 153, 154.

commented that our capacity to wonder before beauty is what convinces us that we are made by and for God. Jean Anouilh remarked that beauty is one of the rare things that do not lead to doubt of God. To live in a reasonable way, I have to believe that the One who is infinite can satisfy my infinite desires for beauty, truth, goodness, etc. Moreover, I have to believe that he desires to satisfy my desires.

All this fills me with great wonder: Where are my desires leading? Are my desires to be trusted? Are they good? Is there some satisfaction for my desires? What is this adventure, this drama of desire all about? My desires suggest to me a thrilling plan—something bigger than myself—and they make me eager to go after it. If we go to the root of our desires, we ascertain that our whole being is propelled toward something full and lasting—to *total* satisfaction. Saint Thomas Aquinas says that a person's life consists in the affection that principally sustains him and in which he finds his greatest satisfaction. And *every* desire plays its part in driving me to that ... in uniting me to Infinity.

I Am Limited

There is another irreducible truth about the human *I* that at first blush can seem a little depressing: I am limited. No matter what I do or how hard I try, I will never be able to bilocate, or read minds, or fly. Not to mention the many, many other menial things that will always be beyond my limited ability (I am pathetic at math; I can't speak foreign languages; I have been and always will be picked last for dodge ball). And not being immaculately conceived, I will always struggle with concupiscence as well as with actual sins. Whatever I am, I need more than what I am. The fact of my shortcomings, my fragility, my defects can be a cause for despair.

Yet, for some reason, I am not despondent over my limitations. Rather, they provoke an important question in me: If I am made by my infinite (and presumably perfect) Maker, then why did he decide to make me imperfect? Either it is a mistake (my *I* doubts that), or there is a reason. Thus, even my limitation has a meaning. My limitation is not my measure. Indeed, the tremendous advantage of my limitations is that they make me depend. They prevent my *I* from folding in on itself, from ceding to the sway of original sin, by prompting me always to rely on the You whose perfection and compassion infinitely exceed my limitations.

Again, we can—and must—verify this from our own experience. For example, if we find ourselves alone and trapped in an elevator, our first and immediate impulse is to start banging on the door as loudly as we can. The terrifying confrontation with our own limitation at that moment persuades us to believe that there is (a) someone who hears our cries; (b) someone who has the ability and the desire to help us; and (c) someone who will actually come to our assistance and rescue us in response to our begging. My experience of limitation makes me a fervent believer in such a powerful Presence overseeing the whole of my life. Without the experience of personal limitation, our faith in such a One could never be so poignant. My limitation convinces me that the answer to what is lacking in me is not to be found in me. Monsignor Luigi Giussani once made the point that the more a person is aware of his limitation and his incapacity, the more he is able to open himself to his answer.

Even more, there is a great benefit to the limitation known as suffering. As Pope John Paul II taught so wondrously, suffering enables us to go beyond ourselves and our pre-conceptions. It makes us aware of the reality of our transcendence. And, no matter how agonizing our suffering may become, nothing can suppress in us that certainty about transcendence elicited by suffering. Suffering gives birth to works of love. Through the experience of suffering, we discover ourselves, our own humanity, our own dignity, our own mission. Leon Bloy has famously stated that man has places in his heart that do not yet exist, and into them enters suffering in order that they may have existence. Just consider how many masterpieces of art were born from the anguish of artists as they confronted their own suffering. The limitation of suffering invites us to manifest the moral greatness of being human. It attests to the spiritual maturity possible for man. The fact that the limitation of suffering contains such a magnificent design makes me wonder about the Designer.

Thanks to the limitation of my *I*, I see how human existence points to something beyond itself as its meaning and goal. My limitation makes me certain of the existence and beneficence of that Beyond. It makes me yearn for it.

I Am Expectation

There is yet one remaining, absolute factor about every human *I*: I expect happiness. I possess no contract, no written guarantee, but something inscribed in the very fiber of my *I* certifies that I have been promised happiness. We live looking for that "thing" that makes life worth living, that gives life consistency, substance, significance. The expectation of happiness exists in me with the force of an inviolable pledge. We are certain that we have a "right" to happiness and fulfillment. In the *Pensees*, Blaise Pascal observes that all persons without exception seek to be happy. Regardless of the means they use, every person at every moment strains toward this goal. He says that the will never takes the least step but toward this object of happiness. This is the motive of all actions of all persons, including those about to hang themselves.[2]

In fact, we feel cheated if happiness does not happen in our lives. We get grumpy ... aggrieved. I do not live for five minutes without pursuing something that will fill this level of being in me. But, just as I cannot adequately fulfill my desires, neither can I make myself happy. Even more, I am not able even *to conceive* of all that I require to be happy. And, as with my desires, I cannot excise this expectation that is identical with my *I*. Expectation is the very structure of my life. I live looking for Something more ... something *totalizing* ... the consummate Something within something. But if I possess an innate expectation for happiness, then it is reasonable for me to conclude that this expectation is meant to be fulfilled. Yet I, left to myself, am not the fullness that I need. And since I cannot satisfy my expectation for completeness, then it only makes sense for me to look to the One who put that expectation in me in the first place—my Maker—in order to find the fulfillment for which my heart languishes.

Once again, the expectation of my *I* for happiness has me looking beyond my *I* to the You who has fashioned me to live with such urgent expectation. The more I contemplate this fact of my *I*, the more I am filled with anticipation and wonder about the happiness that I am sure exists as much as I exist. And my experience tells me that the only thing that will fulfill my heart totally is not a thing at all: it is a Person.

---

[2] Blaise Pascal, *Pensées*, trans. W. F. Trotter (New York: E. P. Dutton and Co., 1958), no. 425.

The Religious Sense

The gravest and most tragic fault is that so many of us do not live our own humanity. We have never done an inventory of the *I*—thus, we live oblivious to it. Even more, we end up neglecting and even undermining our *I*. However, if people are not provoked and educated to an authentic awareness of what it means to be human—of what it means to be an *I*—then they fall prey to merely instinctive impulses in dealing with the various circumstances and situations they face; they react to life instead of responding to it. They become like the person in Zbigniew Herbert's moving but morose poem, "A Life":

I was a quiet boy a little sleepy and—amazingly—
unlike my peers—who were fond of adventures—
I didn't expect much—didn't look out the window
At school more diligent than able—docile stable

Then a normal life at the level of a regular clerk
up early street tram office again tram home sleep

I truly don't know why I'm tired uneasy in torment
perpetually even now—when I have a right to rest

I know I never rose high—I have no achievements
I collected stamps medicinal herbs was OK at chess

I went abroad once—on a holiday to the Black Sea
in the photo a straw hat tanned face—almost happy

I read what came to hand: about scientific socialism
about flights into space and machines that can think
and the thing I liked most: books on the life of bees

Like others I wanted to know what I'd be after death
whether I'd get a new apartment if life had meaning

And above all how to tell the good from what's evil
to know for sure what is white and what's all black

Someone recommended a classic work—as he said
it changed his life and the lives of millions of others
I read it—I didn't change—and I'm ashamed to admit
for the life of me I don't remember the classic's name

Maybe I didn't live but endured—cast against my will
into something hard to govern and impossible to grasp
a shadow on a wall
so it was not a life
a life up to the hilt

How could I explain to my wife or to anyone else
that I summoned all my strength
so as not to commit stupidities cede to insinuation
not to fraternize with the strongest

It's true—I was always pale. Average. At school
in the army in the office at home and at parties

Now I'm in the hospital dying of old age.
Here is the same uneasiness and torment.
Born a second time perhaps I'd be better.

I wake at night in a sweat. Stare at the ceiling. Silence.
And again—one more time—with a bone-weary arm
I chase off the bad spirits and summon the good ones.[3]

It hurts to read that poem. It leaves us wondering: How
could such a barely lived life happen? But the poem under-
scores that it can.

---

[3] Zbigniew Herbert, *The Collected Poems, 1956–1998*, trans. Alissa Valles (New
York: HarperCollins Publishers, 2007), pp. 471–72.

So we undertake a simple yet profound search of self, such as the one we have outlined, in the hope of opening ourselves to ourselves. In considering the nonnegotiable factors of "who we really are", we come away with a certainty about the *I* that constitutes a kind of breakthrough. Because then I realize (perhaps for the first time in my life) that when I use the word "I" of myself, I am referring to a reality that is immeasurable, unquantifiable, that defies reduction—that cannot be minimized to the sum of some attributes or certain personal traits. To say "I" is to refer to something *spiritual* because the *I* is *a relationship* with the Infinite. The assessment we have done has verified it.

When we are honest enough to admit this, then we are struck with wonder. Because then we realize that to be an *I* is to be *wanted* by Someone greater than myself. All the Big Questions that impose themselves on us as we perform our painstaking analysis of our *I* point to an indubitable conclusion: I *belong* to Someone; I am part of a belonging. The more I recognize the truth of my *I*, the more I ascertain that to be an *I* is to be *wanted by God*. This is really the first time in this chapter that we have introduced any explicit discussion of God. And that is on purpose. Because it is only once we have come to terms with the reality of our *I* that the concept of "God" bears any relevance, carries any *correspondence* to me. Only once I broach *the Question that I am* do I care to know *the Answer who is God*. And if I do not live at the level of my *I* than I live by default at the level of an *idol*.

But now the question has been broached. And the whole of my *I*—with excruciating longing that I have never experienced before—cries out for a You. "To be myself I need someone else.... Alone, we cannot be ourselves."[4] This notion has been a prevalent theme in the writings of Pope Benedict XVI. For example, when a cardinal, he wrote: "The I realizes itself through a you. . . ."[5] "The key to the *I* lies with the *thou*; the way to the *thou* leads through the *I.* . . ." "The reason why an individual cannot accept the *thou*, cannot come to terms with him, is that he does not like his own *I* and, for that reason, cannot accept a *thou*."[6]

Once we have confronted reality in this radical way—and it has become patently clear to us that we are always looking for something more . . . that we don't own a measure by which to make sense of everything . . . that all reality points to a beyond which we long to be part of—*and* once we have decided that reality is something we want to stick around for, then we have arrived at what Monsignor Luigi Giussani calls *the religious sense*. Because then, at the deepest level of our consciousness, filled with wonder, we start asking questions—about the ultimate meaning of existence, about why there is pain and suffering, about what reality is made for, about truth. As Giussani brilliantly observes, "If one's understanding of reality could be satiated solely by responding to a thousand questions, and man were to find the answer to the nine hundredth and ninety-ninth, then he would still be as restless and unsatisfied as if he were at the beginning."[7] It's so true!

[4] Luigi Giussani, *At the Origin of the Christian Claim* (Montreal: McGill Queen's University Press, 1998), pp. 95–96.

[5] Joseph Cardinal Ratzinger, *Co-Workers of the Truth* (San Francisco: Ignatius Press, 1992), pp. 82–83.

[6] Joseph Cardinal Ratzinger, *Principles of Catholic Theology*, trans. Sr. Mary Frances McCarthy (San Francisco: Ignatius Press, 1987), pp. 80, 79.

[7] Luigi Giussani, *The Religious Sense* (Montreal: McGill-Queen's University Press, 1997), p. 47.

The religious sense is the compulsion to find the truth of my life in an answer that I am certain is beyond me. The religious sense is that inner driving force that propels me to discover total meaning and satisfaction for the urgent need that I am—and I am convinced that the only adequate answer can be found in Mystery. And because the religious sense is identical with who I am, it interfaces with every act of my life; it determines every choice, every decision, every judgment I make in life. As Monsignor Giussani puts it, "By the very fact that a person lives five minutes he affirms the existence of a 'something' which deep down makes living those five minutes worthwhile." [8] It is the religious sense that keeps us affirming the existence of that something which makes life worth living ... something beyond us—mysterious but absolute and all-encompassing.

The *Catechism* describes the religious sense this way:

> The desire for God is written in the human heart, because man is created by God and for God; and God never ceases to draw man to himself. Only in God will he find the truth and happiness he never stops searching for.... At every time and in every place, God draws close to man. He calls man to seek him, to know him, to love him with all his strength.... Christ comes to meet every human being. It is he who first seeks us.... Man is by nature and vocation a religious being (*CCC* nos. 27, 1, 2560, 44).

To this extent, as Saint Basil the Great observes, the love of God cannot be "taught". He says that men did not need to learn how to rejoice in the presence of light, or to embrace life, or to love our parents and children; much less were we taught the love of God. A certain seminal principle was implanted in us which has within itself the

[8] Ibid., p. 57.

cause by which men cling to God. Basil concludes that God is by nature inherent in us.

Another way of getting at the meaning of the religious sense is from the perspective of "predisposition" as described by Saint Thomas Aquinas: "Since perfect knowledge consists in the divine enjoyment, it was necessary that the affections of man be disposed to desire the divine fruition. Just as we know that there is in man a natural desire for happiness, and the desire for the enjoyment of anything is caused by a love for that thing, so it was necessary that man tending to perfect happiness be led to divine love."[9]

In his *Introduction to Moral Theology*, Father Romanus Cessario, O.P., makes the point that "there are naturally knowable truths, both in doctrine and morals, that serve as preambles to the grace of Christian belief." Then he goes on to cite his fellow Dominican theologian Edward Schillebeeckx, who argued that "if man does not make definite contact with God at one point that is not grace (in the theological sense of the word), then the God who reveals himself cannot address man meaningfully".[10]

The nemesis of our religious sense, as Pope Benedict XVI understands it, is agnosticism because inasmuch as agnosticism "derives from the reduction of human intelligence to a mere practical mechanism", it thereby "tends to stifle the religious sense engraved in the depths of our nature".[11] An awakened religious sense, conversely, is the full-flowering of human intelligence; it is reason's zenith.

---

[9] St. Thomas Aquinas, *Summa Contra Gentiles* IV, 54.

[10] Romanus Cessario, *Introduction to Moral Theology* (Washington, D.C.: The Catholic University of America Press, 2001), p. 11.

[11] Pope Benedict XVI, "Address to the Participants at the Ecclesial Convention of the Diocese of Rome" (June 5, 2006).

This is expressed with eloquent simplicity in James Baldwin's play *Blues for Mister Charlie*:

RICHARD: You know I don't believe in God, Grandmama.

MOTHER: You don't know what you talking about. Ain't no way possible for you not to believe in God. It ain't up to you.... It's up to the life in you—the life in you. *That* knows where it comes from, *that* believes in God.[12]

Here is another way to understand the religious sense: "The most beautiful emotion we can experience is the mysterious. It is the fundamental emotion that stands at the cradle of all true art and science. He to whom this emotion is a stranger, who can no longer wonder and stand rapt in awe, is as good as dead, a snuffed-out candle. To sense that behind anything that can be experienced there is something that our minds cannot grasp, whose beauty and sublimity reaches us only indirectly: this is religiousness." Those words were written by Albert Einstein.[13]

One of the chief purposes of preaching is to animate and educate people's religious sense.

To cry out for God once we have discovered the truth about our own humanity is *the* most reasonable thing we can do. If reason wants to be coherent with itself, it must admit the existence of something greater than itself, something incomprehensible, something beyond all measures ... what is known as *Mystery*. Giussani expresses it this way: "The summit of reason's conquest is the perception of a ... Presence, to which all human movement is destined, because it depends upon it. Mystery is ... reason's greatest discovery.... Human existence as need points to some-

---

[12] James Baldwin, *Blues for Mister Charlie* (New York: Dell, 1964), pp. 33, 34.
[13] "The World as I See It", *Forum and Century* 84 (1930):193–94.

thing beyond itself as its meaning, its goal.... To be conscious of oneself right to the core is to perceive, at the depths of the self, an Other." [14]

When we arrive at the point in which our religious sense is awakened and enlivened, we find ourselves praying with the Psalmist, "Bow your heavens, O LORD, and come down!" (Ps 144:5). And the astounding reality is that *God does!* Yet, when the Son of God comes in the Incarnation and dwells among us, how is it possible that we are able to recognize him as The Answer that we have been looking for all our lives? *Because of a* CORRESPONDENCE *with our experience.*

> If God became man and came among us, recognizing him should be easy. Why is it easy to recognize him? Because of an exceptionality—an exceptionality beyond compare. What does exceptional mean? Why do you feel something "exceptional" to be exceptional? Because it corresponds to the expectations of your heart, no matter how confused and nebulous they might be. It corresponds unexpectedly to the needs of your mind or your heart, to the irresistible, undeniable demands of your heart in a way you could never have imagined or predicted, because there is no one like this man.... It is the exceptionality with which the figure of Christ appears that makes it easy to recognize him. [15]

But before exploring the implications of all this for preaching, one final caution from Giussani: "It would be impossible to become fully aware of what Jesus Christ means if one did not first become fully aware of the nature of

---

[14] Giussani, *Religious Sense*, pp. 117, 115, 106.

[15] Luigi Giussani, "Recognizing Christ: The First Accents of a New Morality", in *Communion and Liberation: A Movement in the Church*, ed. Davide Rondoni, trans. Patrick Stevenson and Susan Scott (Montreal: McGill-Queens, 2000), pp. 12–13.

that dynamism which makes a person human. Christ proposes himself as the answer to what 'I' am, and only an attentive, tender, and impassioned awareness of my own self can make me open and lead me to acknowledge, admire, thank, and live Christ."[16]

The Implications for Preaching

What does all this have to do with preaching? For the sake of clarity, we will number the primary ramifications of what we have covered. These seven points represent the chief principles in our approach to preaching that we will revisit again and again throughout the book.

1. The principal duty of the preacher is to reactivate and educate the religious sense of his hearers. The religious sense is reenergized in people, not by way of an ethical choice or a lofty idea, but through the *happening* of the Event of Christ—the preacher offers "the announcement of a happening that surprises mankind in the same way in which, two thousand years ago, the announcement of the angels in Bethlehem surprised poor shepherds.... It's the perception of this happening that revives or strengthens the elementary sense of dependence and the core of original evidence to which we give the name of 'religious sense'."[17] Take note, though, that the preacher can reawaken the religious sense of others only if he is alert and sensitive to the active urging of the religious sense in his own life.

---

[16] Giussani, *At the Origin of the Christian Claim*, p. 6.
[17] Interview with Luigi Giussani by Angelo Scola (1987).

2.   The preacher educates the religious sense in others by revealing to people the truths of their own *I*. In so doing, he provokes the Big Questions that are identical with what it means to be human. In terms of method, the preacher's first purpose is simply to coax people to acknowledge facts about themselves (Who They Are!) that they may have forgotten, neglected, or never known. The preacher's intention is to invite people back to an attentive, tender, and impassioned awareness of their own selves that in turn makes them open to Something More.

3.   In bringing people to an attentive awareness of their *I*, the preacher entices them to trust their elementary experience—their heart. He moves them to explore their insuperable need for love, beauty, truth, goodness, justice, and happiness. For the heart is the only adequate way to approach reality. We compare everything we come in contact with to our elementary experience in order to make a judgment about whether a given thing is good and valuable for us. Preaching is about reconciliation, and the first thing that has to be reunited is the hearer with his elementary experience.

4.   But many hearts have been broken. Many people have opted to distract, anesthetize, encrust, or repress their hearts. Many have caved in to the nihilism of original sin. Yet the evidence of their persistent discontentment, of their prevailing miserableness, confirms how erroneous it is to hazard identifying the total value of everything with some aspect of ourselves. The infallible heart keeps on yearning for what only *it* knows corresponds to it. And what it awaits is greater than

anything we could possibly manufacture or comprehend. Don't lose heart over the scheming of original sin; just remember the melancholy man in the poem who admits:

I truly don't know why I'm tired uneasy in torment
perpetually even now....
Like others I wanted to know ... if life had meaning
And above all how to tell the good from what's evil....
Born a second time perhaps I'd be better.

Your preaching will give those in the grip of original sin the chance to be born a second time. As he lies in the hospital bed summoning good spirits, he is waiting for you.

5.   The preacher must offer his hearers *a proposal*—a proposal that is an appropriate response to *a lived question* in the hearers. For if the preacher has been successful in breaking through the subterfuge of original sin, if he has managed to move people to embrace the truth of their *I* and to approach reality starting from the perspective of their elementary experience, then people will require at that moment a concrete Gospel proposal that *they can compare with their hearts*—something that excites, edifies, and enlarges them. Preaching is not indoctrination; it solicits the freedom of the *I* of the hearer. That is why it is so vital for the preacher's proposal to address *a lived question* in his hearers, that is, a question that engages his hearers fully and directly at the level of their *I*. The preacher's proposal must implicate the "problem" that men are: they are a thirst for truth and meaning that they themselves cannot satisfy (in this sense we *are* a structural disproportion).

For this reason, nothing academic or theoretical will do. Preaching that does not proceed from experience by posing a lived question will be promptly dismissed as abstract, irrelevant, annoying, forgettable, infuriating, and, ultimately, insulting.

6. To equip the preacher in this task, God has provided his Church with Sacred Scripture. As the preacher begins the process of preparing to preach by way of the irreplaceable first step of praying over the Scriptures, his *lectio divina* leads him to ask certain key questions of the text: How does this Scripture respond to the elementary needs of those who will hear it? What does it reveal that leads to a deeper understanding of the *I*? In what way does it provoke the religious sense? What concretely does it propose as an answer to the urgent questions of the human heart? The genius of Sacred Scripture is that it offers not simply a message but rather a divine and life-giving Presence. In other words, the preacher looks for the *correspondence* between what the Scripture offers and what the human heart is begging for. Like the game *Jeopardy*, we preachers read the Scripture identifying the Answer, but what we speak aloud is the corresponding question—that's the key to winning.

7. Be mindful that what people expect to recognize in preaching is an exceptional Presence that corresponds to their hearts—a Presence that answers their burning yearning and that moves them to say Yes to the preacher's proposal. The preacher in the exceptionality of his person (configured to Christ) becomes the correspondence by which people recognize Christ. It is what

Saint Paul means when he says in First Corinthians 11:1, "Be imitators of me, as I am of Christ."

Applying the Method: A Practical Example

How does all this play out in an actual example? Perhaps the ideal paradigm for preaching in the Gospels is Christ's encounter with the Samaritan woman at the well—John 4:1–30, 39–42. (Throughout the book we will use this episode to illustrate various essential points about preaching.) Let us look at this account to see how the method applies concretely in practice.

To begin, the very first thing that Jesus does when he comes face to face with the woman at the well is to take stock of her situation. He can tell that she is in distress. The fact that she is alone at the hottest time of day collecting water indicates that there is something seriously wrong, something amiss. The starting point of Christ's preaching is to address that experience of hers.

Notice that when Jesus lays eyes on the Samaritan woman he does not begin by saying: I am the Son of God— the answer to all your troubles, to everything you need (even though he is). Rather, he makes an assessment of the want that is most pressing on the woman's *I*—the thing in her experience that most immediately impinges on her need for fulfillment/happiness.

The most pressing issue appears to be the woman's need for water. In response, Jesus offers her "living water"— that is, he promises the thing that most provokes her elementary experience. The woman wants water that will slake her bodily thirst once and for all ... but Christ sees in this thirst an indication of the greater existential thirst symbolized. Just as the woman cannot deny her physical thirst (hence she goes after the water), neither can she successfully deny her thirst for happiness/fulfillment . . . although she may try to repress it, ignore it. Christ intends to reunite her to her experience. That is precisely what the dialogue about the living water provokes.

The provocation works. In a small way, the woman *expresses a desire*—"Sir, give me this water"—which means that in some way her *I* has been engaged. She is ready to compare what Christ has to offer with her heart (her elementary experience).

But Jesus realizes how compromised her *I* has become as a result of past and present sin. He exposes it—not to condemn the woman—but rather to assure her just how total and far-reaching is the mercy that Jesus offers. He must lay bare her *I* to its depths, because it is only at the level of the *I* that the woman can be engaged, that she can hear the proposal made to a lived question posed directly to her *I*, and that she can respond with a fully free Yes.

At first the woman is evasive, but Christ's presence invites her back to an attentive, tender, and impassioned awareness of her self. She is reunited with her heart. Her *I* is alive. She faces the demands of her heart; she goes to the root of her desires. The religious sense burns in her so much that she declares, "I know a Messiah is coming." By her credo, the woman confesses that she is looking for the ultimate meaning and fulfillment of her life in something that exceeds her reason and resources: she is looking for Mystery, for the culmination of the relationship with the Infinite that she knows in her heart that she is.

And now, Jesus Christ—who has provoked a Lived Question in a woman who formerly was divorced from her own *I* (as well as from a number of men) . . . who was separated from her own elementary experience (even though her life was obsessed with thirst) ... who began her exchange with Christ by calling him by no title at all but then concluded their conversation by calling him "the Messiah"—gives her the Answer she has been looking for all her life (especially in the relationships with men that were not enough to satisfy the infinite needs of her heart). Only infinity is enough for her. And so Jesus says: "I who speak to you am he." The exceptionality of his Presence, which is ordered specifically to her heart, creates an instantaneous correspondence. The woman goes off into the town converted and converting: at her words, the people in the town set out to meet Jesus. In *this sinful woman*, they experience an exceptionality that so corresponds to their own hearts that they immediately want to go and meet what she has met!

And so the process begins again.

Take a look at the way then–Cardinal Ratzinger's stunning evaluation of Christ's encounter with the woman at the well sums up so many of the salient points that we have considered:

> The account of Jesus' meeting with the Samaritan woman at Jacob's well opens with the meeting of Jesus and the Samaritan woman in the context of a normal, human, everyday experience—the experience of thirst, which is surely one of man's most primordial experiences. In the course of the conversation, the subject shifts to that thirst that is a thirst for life, and the point is made that one must drink again and again, must come again and again to the source. In this way, the woman is made aware of what in actuality she, like every human being, has always known but to which she has not always adverted: that she thirsts for life itself and that all the assuaging that she seeks and finds cannot satiate this living, elemental thirst. The superficial "empirical" experience has been transcended....

There comes to light the real dilemma, the deep-seated waywardness, of her existence: she is brought face to face with herself. In general, we can reduce what is happening to the formula: one must know oneself as one really is if one is to know God. The real medium, the primordial experience of all experiences, is that man himself is the place in which and through which he experiences God. . . . The woman stands face to face with herself. It is no longer a question now *of something* but of the depths of the *I* itself and, consequently, of the radical poverty that *is* man's I-myself. . . . In the moment in which this occurs, the question of all questions arises always and of necessity: the question about oneself becomes a question about God. . . . Only at this point does the offering of Jesus' true gift become possible. . . . Now the woman is aware of the real thirst by which she is driven. Hence she can at last learn what it is for which this thirst thirsts. It is the purpose and meaning of all catechesis to lead to this thirst. . . . Catechesis must lead to self-knowledge, to the exposing of the *I*, so that it lets the masks fall and moves out of the realm *of something* into that of being. Its goal is *conversio*, that conversion of man that results in his standing face to face with himself. . . . *Conversio* is the way in which man finds himself.[18]

Conclusion

Pope John Paul II wrote that "the priest as minister of the Word 'must always be *a man of knowledge* in the highest and most religious sense of the term. He must possess and pass on that 'knowledge of God' which is not a mere deposit of doctrinal truths but a personal and living experience of the Mystery." [19] And a instruction issued by the Congregation for the Clergy makes this claim:

[18] Ratzinger, *Principles of Catholic Theology*, pp. 353–55.
[19] Pope John Paul II, *Gift and Mystery* (New York: Image Books, 1996), p. 95.

The Gospel preached by the Church is not just a message but *a divine and life-giving experience* for those who believe, hear, receive, and obey the message.... In hearing the Word, *the actual encounter with God* himself calls to the heart of man and demands a decision which is not arrived at solely through the intellectual knowledge but which requires conversion of heart.... The proclamation of the Gospel by the sacred ministers of the Church is, in a certain sense, *a participation in the salvific character of the Word itself.*[20]

It is time to turn our attention to *encounter.*

---

[20] Congregation for the Clergy, *The Priest and the Third Christian Millennium, Teacher of the Word, Minister of the Sacraments, and Leader of the Community* (1999), 2.1; emphasis added.

CHAPTER 2

The Method:

Preaching Is an Encounter

"I ... was unable to be free within myself, until the day of my encounter with him through whose Presence I was born to myself."

— Fr. Maurice Zundel

September 25, 2000, was the day the voices got to be too much for him. John Kevin Hines was a nineteen-year-old college freshman from San Francisco. According to the news reports, for a long time Hines had suffered from mental illness. The voices in his head told him to take his own life. And finally Hines could resist them no longer. So that morning, he kissed his father on the cheek, boarded a local bus, and headed to the Golden Gate Bridge where he would carry out his plan to end his life. He was going to jump off the bridge. As he sat on the bus, he was crying. But ... he told himself that if anyone asked him what was wrong, he would not go through with it.

No one did.

Hines got to the bridge, walked midway across it, and stood looking down at the water for forty minutes ... waiting. At that point, a tourist wearing sunglasses approached him and asked: "Would you take my picture?" Hines snapped her picture ... then took a few steps back, rushed the railing, and threw himself over.

The moment he began his plunge to the waters 220 feet below, he regretted it, saying to himself: "What did I just do? I don't want to die." We know this because—miraculously—Hines survived, thank God.

That chilling account gives us pause. As we reflect on it, a terrible truth becomes evident: only one little thing was needed to prevent that suffering young man from throwing away his life. And what was that? A *presence*. By his own admission, all Hines was waiting for was for someone—really anyone—simply to take notice and to speak to him with concern. That simple solicitude could have saved his life.

Preaching exists in the Church to be a life-saving presence that reaches out to those in peril and that rescues them from their despair, their demise.

Our Need for a Presence

There is a disturbing passage in the memoirs of the nineteenth-century French composer Hector Berlioz. He wrote, "It is difficult to put into words what I suffered—the longing that seemed to be tearing my heart out by the roots, the dreadful sense of being alone in an empty universe.... I suffered agonies and lay groaning on the ground, stretching out abandoned arms, convulsively tearing up handfuls of grass and wide-eyed innocent daisies, struggling against the crushing sense of *absence*, against a mortal isolation." [1] How many of the people to whom we preach

[1] Hector Berlioz, *The Memoirs of Hector Berlioz*, trans. David Cairns (New York: Alfred A. Knopf, 1969), pp. 120–21, 190.

suffer under the weight of such oppression? The dread of "mortal isolation" seems almost epidemic.

We cannot abide absence. Solitariness, being without genuine companionship, living without belonging: all of this speaks to the most menacing of human torments; in fact, Pope Benedict XVI refers to loneliness as an analogy for hell. Preaching in the Church exists first to be a companion to those whose seclusion impedes them from living the risk of their own lives. Notice that John Kevin Hines was not looking for a message or some counsel to deter him from going through with his suicidal plan; all he needed was someone to be personally present to him with compassion. This is the preacher.

The Presence offered by way of presence via the preacher enables us to become ourselves. In the words of that now celebrated passage from *Gaudium et Spes* (no. 22), "Only in the mystery of the incarnate Word does the mystery of man take on light. Christ ... fully reveals man to man himself." Father Julián Carrón has made the point that we are not ourselves without a Presence to help us, lending us a hand so that our *I* be constantly awakened, so that freedom can truly adhere. We need a Presence that will free us above all from "the decay of ourselves". How many of us experience that decay on a daily basis. This is why Giussani insists that that for which the *I* is made and for which it does everything is a Presence.

In his book *Introduction to Christianity*, written even before he was a bishop, Joseph Ratzinger, in order to emphasize this vital role of presence, points to the example of a very common phobia: the fear of being alone in a room with a corpse. He says that a person who has to keep watch alone in a room with a dead person feels fear, even though that person knows perfectly well that the cadaver can do no harm. In fact, the situation would be more dangerous if the person in question were still alive. The then–Father Ratzinger asks,

> How ... can such fear be overcome if proof of its groundlessness has no effect? Well, the child will lose his fear the moment that there is a hand there to take him and lead him, and a voice to talk to him; at the moment therefore at which he experiences the fellowship of a loving human being. Similarly, he who is alone with the corpse will feel the bout of fear recede when there is a human being with him, when he experiences the nearness of a "You".... The fear peculiar to man cannot be overcome by reason but only by the presence of someone who loves him.[2]

How very many people today face life with this kind of fear and foreboding? For them the whole of life is like being alone in a room with a corpse. It is so important for the preacher to realize, even before opening his mouth to speak, that his presence represents the offer of a loving hand, which the fearful can grasp and follow. The preacher's presence as *alter Christus* offers the loving fellowship of a You. Before all else, preaching is Christ's nearness.

It is essential for the preacher to understand and embrace this aspect of preaching before any actual homily-giving begins. The twentieth-century Catholic philosopher Louis Lavelle makes a key observation about fallen human nature: "Every man instinctively resists the influence which another attempts to wield over him." All the same, "every person responds with total confidence and joy to one who would draw him towards an invisible presence, a presence from which he draws strength; for when another makes him aware of it, that presence ceases to be an illusion, a fiction,

---

[2] Joseph Ratzinger, *Introduction to Christianity*, trans. J. R. Foster, 2nd ed. (San Francisco: Ignatius Press, 2004), p. 299.

or a mere hope, and becomes the very presence of the living God." [3] And this is the seminal role of the preacher as it is rooted in the very preaching of Christ. "Jesus' proclamation", then–Cardinal Ratzinger asserts, "was never mere preaching, mere words; it was 'sacramental', in the sense that his words were and are inseparable from his 'I'—from his 'flesh'." [4]

The presence that we expect in preaching, then, is "real"—it is efficacious. As Father Julián Carrón puts it, "A real presence is needed, so attractive as to sweep all our affection along with it. This bond cannot be established by any rule: no ethic, no spiritualism can do it. What is needed is the *event of a presence* that so corresponds that it can overcome all our resistance." [5] Or again, in the words of then Cardinal Ratzinger: "What we need is the presence in our lives of what is real and permanent so that we can approach it." [6] And that presence is made available to us by way of an *encounter*.

Being Christian Is the Result of an Encounter

Louis Lavelle leads us back to the authority of our own elementary experience in order to help us recognize the signal instrumentality of encounter in our lives. He writes:

> The most significant event in the lives of most of us has almost always been an encounter with another human being who suddenly threw new light upon our lives, changed

---

[3] Louis Lavelle, *The Dilemma of Narcissus* (Burdett: Larson Publications, 1993), pp. 164–65.

[4] Joseph Cardinal Ratzinger, *Gospel, Catechesis, Catechism: Sidelights on the "Catechism of the Catholic Church"* (San Francisco: Ignatius Press, 1997), p. 50.

[5] Quoted in Communion and Liberation, *Event of Freedom: Exercises of the Fraternity of Communion and Liberation* (Rimini, 2003), p. 23.

[6] Joseph Cardinal Ratzinger, *The Feast of Faith: Approaches to a Theology of the Liturgy* (San Francisco: Ignatius Press, 1986), pp. 150–51.

its direction and meaning, gave it balance and an inflec-
tion that it had hitherto been unable to achieve. It is not
necessary to have lived with this person in long familiar-
ity to attain such a result. A very brief contact can be sufficient. True influence is that of *pure presence;* it is the
discovery of one's own being through contact with another
being.[7]

We simply have to reflect on our own lives to verify this.
A relative, a teacher, a coach, a mentor, a classmate, a
friend, someone who offered us counsel, correction, criticism, or advice may come to mind. We can readily connect the "discovery of our own being" with a concrete
encounter with another person.

Why is encounter so integral to Christianity and to the
proposal of Christianity? Because, as Monsignor Romano
Guardini pointed out almost one hundred years ago, the
essence of Christianity is not an *idea* but a *Person.* Encounter is God's very *method* of salvation. This conviction is the
resounding central claim on the first page of the first encyc-
lical of Pope Benedict XVI, *Deus Caritas Est.* "Being Christian is not the result of an ethical choice or a lofty idea, but
the encounter with an event, a person, which gives life a
new horizon and a decisive direction." [8] Pope Benedict's
declaration is a confirmation and intensification of a similar point that Pope John Paul II had previously made:

Man never stops seeking: both when he is marked by the
drama of violence, loneliness, and insignificance, and when
he lives in serenity and joy, he continues to seek. The only
answer which can satisfy him and appease this search of

[7] Louis Lavelle, *Evil and Suffering,* trans. Bernard Murchland (New York: The
Macmillan Co., 1963), p. 137.

[8] Benedict XVI, *God Is Love,* Deus Caritas Est, no. 1 (San Francisco: Ignatius Press, 2006), p. 7.

his comes from the encounter with the One who is at the source of his being and his action. . . . Christ is the Way, the Truth, and the Life, who reaches the person in his day-to-day existence. The discovery of this road normally comes about through the mediation of other human beings. Marked through the gift of faith by the encounter with the Redeemer, believers are called to become an echo of the event of Christ, to become themselves an "event." Christianity, even before being a sum of doctrines or a rule for salvation, is thus the "event" of an encounter.[9]

When the angel Gabriel appeared to the Blessed Virgin Mary at the Annunciation, what transpired was an encounter by which the Word became flesh in Mary's womb. Mary did not say Yes in response to an ethical choice posed by the angel or to some lofty idea he floated (maybe literally). The Blessed Virgin's *fiat* was the result of an encounter with an Event, a Person that gave her life—and subsequently our life—a new horizon, a decisive direction. Every time we pray the Angelus, we do not simply recall some communiqué given and received. Rather, we engage in a re-happening of that encounter in order to retrieve for our life here and now the promised new horizon, the decisive direction we require. Our prayer is a way of re-presenting the event of that saving encounter so that the reality of that Divine Presence will take effect and become normative in our lives.

Hans Urs von Balthasar offers a beautiful description of the all-encompassing importance of encounter:

In order to gain an insight into humanity, the individual must encounter an *other*. The human being exists only in

[9] Pope John Paul II, "Letter to Msgr. Luigi Giussani on the Occasion of the 50th Anniversary of the Movement 'Communion and Liberation'" (February 22, 2004).

relation to others; he truly *is* only in the reciprocity of an I and Thou. The otherness of the other is a fundamental fact that he must acknowledge if there is to be any possibility of forming a harmonious community in the commonality of human nature.... Man sustains himself—indeed, he first comes to himself—in an encounter. When one man meets another face to face, truth comes to pass, the depths of human existence come to light spontaneously, in freedom and in grace.... The two [become] joined in a truth that transcends their finitude.... If God, the Wholly-Other, ever wishes to encounter man, the place he manifests himself cannot but lie in the person who remains ever "other" to me, in other words, my "neighbor".[10]

What is so unique about an encounter that it can bring all this about? An encounter is an interaction with another that provokes a question, and the question is, "What are you looking for?" At the very moment that that question gets raised in us, we realize that the answer is to be found in the person we are encountering. This is the dynamic at work in the phenomenon of "love at first sight". And when the encounter in question is an encounter with Jesus Christ, then Christ offers himself, his Person, as the Answer to the question "What are you looking for?"—the question that defines our *I* and that drives our religious sense.

How do we know if we have had an encounter (for not every meeting with another person is necessarily an encounter)? There are certain verifying signs. An encounter is something unexpected and surprising. We are struck by the "something different" of an encounter that makes an indelible impact on us with its newness, freshness, and value. Despite the passing of time, a true encounter never loses its attraction for us. We cannot erase an encounter

[10] Hans Urs von Balthasar, *Love Alone Is Credible* (San Francisco: Ignatius Press, 2005), pp. 43–44, 45, 46–47.

from our souls because it implicates the whole person; it reaches to the roots of all the Big Questions of our *I*. We come away from an encounter with a new way of looking at things, for an encounter opens wide the whole of our *I*. It energizes our reason and imbues us with wonder. Through a genuine encounter our hearts can somehow perceive the exceptional meaning offered; we can "see inside" an encounter. Thanks to an encounter, our freedom adheres easily to the answer we find in the other (like Mary's Yes to the angel), for through the efficacy of an encounter we become imbued with self-knowledge and graced with strength to face life anticipating its meaningfulness. An encounter augments us so much that we are no longer inhibited by our fragility; rather, the encounter "launches" us. The joy of an encounter makes us want to stay with the person we have met, to live a relationship with that person, to embrace whatever is important to that person and to make it our own.

Preaching is meant to be all that! If the possibility of being Christian is contingent on an encounter with a Person who gives life a new horizon, then it is crucial that preaching be conceived of and carried out as an encounter. To approach preaching in any other way amounts to reducing it to an abstraction. No matter how doctrinally perfect or brilliantly insightful it may be, it misses the point. For only an encounter turns people into Christians. The Truth we are looking for has to be a *Person*, not a message. Preaching is not speech-making; it is not a discourse. Preaching is like trying to describe some phenomenal play at a baseball game. In trying to recapture the amazing happening for someone who did not see it, we use an appropriate style and only as many words as are needed to re-create the event in such a way that the other can experience it.

But all this seems too much. How can we preachers possibly accomplish it? Well ... the effects of an encounter happen when the preacher returns again and again to what happened *to himself* personally. (This is the reason for prayer.) Preaching is about re-presenting What Happened. It is an event. By "event" we mean something new and unforeseen that occurs, provoking surprise and wonder. An event awakens us and makes us alert. We can't resist it—an event stays with us. A friend of mine in speaking about the birth of his youngest son said, "It is an event in the past that doesn't belong there"; he said this because every day the event of that birth animates and changes my friend. It impinges upon his life in every conceivable way. An event is the introduction of something new that keeps on making things new. The reason why we woke up believing in God today is because of an Event that has taken hold of us and kept us faithful. Preaching is an event that mediates The Event. The encounter that is Gospel preaching proceeds from the preacher's own first encounter with the Event who is Jesus Christ as well as from the daily encounters that renew that first Event and amplify it.

Preaching as Encounter: New Testament Examples

Encounter constitutes the very structure of Scripture, especially the New Testament. One of the most prominent Scripture scholars in the United States, Father Francis Martin, has isolated out of the various narrative forms within the Gospels a distinctive form that he calls the "encounter story". Martin writes that encounter stories

> continue, by way of representation, those gestures of Jesus by which he revealed God's care for the poor, the sinners, the sick, the marginal people of man-made society. These

narrative actions do not only speak of this care, but *they make it present* by the literary reenactment of Jesus' activity. . . . The Gospel encounter stories . . . are efficacious "testimony narratives" bearing witness not only to what Jesus did *but also to what he is doing*. They are a word of witness in the Church, made living and active by the anointing action of the Holy Spirit, so that for those who receive their literary action in faith, *they become the source of an encounter with Jesus now*, as being the one who heals, calls to discipleship, and enlightens. . . . The intention of the Gospel narrations of this type is that *of portraying the person of Jesus* as endowed with the power to bring about the resolution of the situations with which he is faced.[11]

Among the many encounter stories in the Gospels, Father Martin lists: the healing of Peter's mother-in-law; the healing of the leper; the exorcism of the demoniac at Capernaum; the raising of the widow of Nain's son; the stilling of the storm; the cursing of the fig tree; the call of James and John/Peter and Andrew; the healings of the centurion's servant, the daughter of Jairus, and the woman with the flow of blood; the healing of the blind man; the healing of the paralytic; the wedding feast of Cana; the woman caught in adultery; the rich young man; the healing of the man with the withered hand . . . and the list goes on.

Let us look at some specific examples of preaching as encounter in the New Testament. It is not a coincidence that the first words of Jesus Christ in the Gospel of John are a sermon-question posed to potential disciples. The question is *the* question: "What do you seek?" (Jn 1:38). This meeting with Jesus is an encounter. The proof that the original encounter never lost its attraction for Andrew and the other disciple with the passing of the years is the fact

[11] Francis Martin, *Encounter Story: A Characteristic Gospel Narrative Form* (Washington, D.C.: Mother of God Services, 1979), pp. 10, 23; emphasis added.

that the *actual time* of the encounter is recorded ("It was about the tenth hour [four in the afternoon]", Jn 1:39). Every day at four o'clock the indelible impact of that first encounter with Christ happened for the disciples again.

Christ's two-word sermon to Matthew—"Follow me" (Mt 9:9)—is an encounter. With that utterance, Matthew's *I* becomes wide open. Despite the paucity of words, Matthew sees inside this gesture of Jesus Christ. He has a new way of looking at things, a radically converted perspective. His whole being is implicated in the way that Christ comes face to face with him. No more for him the vice-laden life of tax collecting/extortion. The encounter with Christ launches Matthew's true self. He gets up and follows Jesus—his newly forged freedom easily adhering to the Presence that overcomes all his inhibitions, all his compromises, his former malice. Thanks to the encounter, Matthew resolves to stay with the One he has met.

The preaching of Christ to Zacchaeus also is not lengthy: "Zacchaeus, make haste and come down; for I must stay at your house today." (Lk 19:5). And yet with those words Zacchaeus is galvanized. Zacchaeus had been trying to see what Jesus was like, and because of this encounter, Zacchaeus met something different that made an unforgettable impression on him. This small-of-stature man is no longer inhibited by his limitations. He hurries down filled with resolve to make restitution, to befriend the poor. Zacchaeus' entire person has been implicated through the encounter—even the darkest parts of his soul. He has a whole new, rectified way of looking at things. The crowd grumbles over Christ's choice of a tax collector for a host, but Zacchaeus has been given a self-knowledge that transcends their pettiness—the reductive way they measure reality according to their own self-imposed standards. Jesus wants to stay at Zacchaeus' house, and Zacchaeus wants to stay with Jesus ... all because of an encounter.

It is easy to see how all the effects of an encounter play out when the Samaritan woman meets Jesus Christ at the well. The first thing that strikes her is that Jesus is "something different"—a Jewish man asking a Samaritan and a woman for a drink. Big Questions come out because of the encounter ... and it is the woman who raises them: Where will you get living water? You can't be greater than Jacob, can you? With these questions, we witness the opening of the woman's *I*, the rousing of her reason, the sparking of wonder. One can trace the progress of the encounter taking hold by noting the titles that the woman uses to address Jesus: she begins, rudely, addressing him with no title at all— she just refers to him as "a Jew"; then she calls him "Sir" (three times—a word that also means "Lord"); then she calls him "a prophet"; finally she calls him "the Messiah". Even having her shameful sins exposed does not make her feel condemned in front of this man. Rather, imbued with a liberating self-knowledge that the encounter has imparted, she races off to share with the others the meaningfulness of life about which she is now convinced. So "launched" is the woman that her sole purpose for going to the well in the first place is abandoned (the water jar). Then a minor miracle happens: the woman's presence to the townspeople becomes an encounter in itself. The people eagerly listen to this woman whom formerly they would have dismissed outright as a good-for-nothing harlot. Filled with wonder, *they* then set out from town to meet Jesus; that encounter moves them to adhere to the Person of Christ, whom they have met through the encounter with the woman.

Peter was the apostle who denied Jesus Christ three times. But the preachment in the form of a thrice-posed question

(Jn 21:15–19) is an encounter that completely transforms the formerly cowardly, unfaithful disciple. All we have to do is turn the page of the Bible to see Peter's transfiguration. As he stands (with John) before the lame man daily placed at the Beautiful Gate of the temple (Acts 3:1–26), he fixes his gaze on the man and commands him, "Look at us!" The crippled man, we are told, gave Peter and John his whole attention in the hope of getting something. But what he experiences is something *different*. Peter promises the man, not silver or gold, but "what he has": the name of Jesus Christ and the power it contains. Peter pulls the man to his feet, restores his *I*, imbues him with wonder and delight, and enables him to face life in a whole new, lasting way. And the healed man, who now can run, does not run off. Instead, he goes with Peter and John into the temple—walking, jumping, and praising God. He has received more than simply his health back. He wants to stay with the apostles . . . with Christ.

One more (though we could go on and on): in Acts 20:17–37, Paul preaches in Miletus to the presbyters of Ephesus. His words are frank, direct, even a little severe. But he concludes by commending his hearers to the Lord and "to the word of his grace, which is able to build you up". The response of the people is that of weeping without restraint. They throw their arms around Paul and kiss him, deeply distressed at the prospect of never seeing his face again. As candid as Paul's words are, his final sermon is an encounter that will never leave them, that will always form the way they look at reality, that will fill them with conviction that life is meaningful, and that their union with Paul can never be severed no matter how many miles may come between them. In fact, the literary elements of this narrative closely resemble Jesus' farewell discourse in the Gospel of John—a patterning that is not coincidental.

An instruction published by the Pontifical Biblical Commission in 1993 entitled *The Interpretation of the Bible in the Church* confirms what we have been proposing: "The presentation of the Gospels should be done in such a way as to elicit an encounter with Christ who provides the key to the whole biblical revelation and communicates the call of God that summons each one to respond" (IV.C.3). Such an encounter with Christ is what enables us to see things as they really are.

Father Stefano Alberto summarizes our findings on "encounter":

> The "I" finds itself again, not thanks to reasoning, not thanks to reflecting on itself, but only through an encounter with a living human reality.... What does "encounter" mean in this instant? It is a "being different" that draws us. It is a being different that attracts, because it corresponds to my heart.... The encounter with Christ, the encounter with this difference that attracts, makes me aware of what I am, what I want. It makes me realize that I am a demand for meaning. It makes me realize that I am desire for happiness. And it makes me realize that what this encounter brings, what this man brings, is what I want. It clarifies my need. The exceptionality of the encounter, the exceptionality of the answer, clarifies my question.[12]

The Implications for Preaching

Let us synopsize what has been said about presence and encounter so that it will be useful and practical for the

---

[12] Stefano Alberto, "The 'I' and the Revolution of the Faith", *Traces* 8, no. 3 (2006): 51–52.

purposes of preaching (again numbering the points for the sake of clarity):

1. Our experience tells us that only a presence is adequate for overcoming our most extreme fear. From time to time, we all experience the crushing sense of absence, the longing that seems to tear our hearts out by the roots—and this can be answered only by a presence. Reason will not suffice to overcome the dread that paralyzes people. That is why God sends his people preachers. Preaching is a way of being present to those whose lives so often fall into the abyss of "mortal isolation".

2. People look to the preacher to see the presence from which *he* draws his strength; that recognition overcomes their resistance. In the preacher, the Church provides a presence that people can approach in order to find their way to God's Presence. The preacher, then, is called to conceive of preaching as an offer of pastoral companionship. The very familiar way in which many of the saints of the early Church preached— such as Saint Augustine and Saint John Chrysostom— may strike us as oddly down-to-earth. They preached without a text in front of them, usually seated, and often engaging in a lively dialogue with the congregation that even managed to incorporate the noises and distractions going on outside the church building during the homily. The new modification to the revised *General Instruction to the Roman Missal*—"The priest, standing at the chair or at the ambo itself *or, when appropriate, in another suitable place*, gives the homily" (no. 136; emphasis added)—seems ordered to

accommodating the personalized presence of the priest-preacher to the congregation.

3. The offer of presence in preaching takes the form of an encounter because the possibility of being Christian is itself the result of an encounter with the Person of Christ. The unchanging method that God has chosen to communicate his life to us is that of encounter—that is why preaching is a participation in this method. As Pope John Paul II impressed upon a group of American bishops during their *ad limina Apostolorum* visit: "The living center of your preaching of the Gospel is the encounter with our Lord himself" (June 4, 2004).

4. It is the purpose of every homily and sermon to pose to the hearers a cardinal question: What are you looking for? The answer that the preacher offers is the Person of Jesus Christ (and not merely his message, his teaching, his moral example, etc.). In the words of then–Cardinal Ratinger:

> Christianity is an ever new encounter, an event thanks to which we can encounter the God who speaks to us, who approaches us, who befriends us. . . . It is critical to come to this fundamental point of a personal encounter with God, who also today makes himself present, and who is contemporary. . . . If this encounter is not realized, which touches the heart, all the rest remains like a weight, almost like something absurd.[13]

5. In order for preaching to be an encounter, the preacher himself must be living out of his own real, actuating

[13] Joseph Cardinal Ratzinger, "Cardinal Ratzinger Tells Why Many Misperceive Christianity", *Zenit* (May 7, 2004): www.zenit.org/article-1033?l=english.

encounter with Jesus Christ. Hence, the preacher constantly returns to and begins from that Event—from *what happened.* To begin from anything other than the preacher's own encounter with Christ is to reduce preaching to an abstraction. The 1982 National Conference of Catholic Bishops (NCCB) document entitled *Fulfilled in Your Hearing: The Homily in the Sunday Assembly* reports that when a survey was taken among a certain group of parishioners about what they hoped to experience during a sermon, what the majority wanted was "simply to hear a person of faith speaking".[14]

Josef Pieper makes the fascinating point that

> in all belief, the decisive factor is *who it is* whose statement is assented to; by comparison the subject matter assented to is in a certain sense secondary. If we pursue this consistently, it follows that belief itself is not yet "purely" achieved when someone accepts as truth the statement of one whom he trusts, but only when he accepts it for the simple reason that *the trusted person states it.* ... The will of the believer is directed toward *the person of the witness.*[15]

Whatever is attractive to the preacher about his encounter with Christ is what is preeminently attractive to others. If the whole of the preacher's *I* is implicated in what he proposes in his preaching, then his preaching will become a true encounter for his hearers.

---

[14] National Conference of Catholic Bishops, *Fulfilled in Your Hearing: The Homily in the Sunday Assembly* (Washington, D.C.: U.S. Catholic Conference, 1982), p. 15.

[15] Josef Pieper, *Faith, Hope, Love*, trans. Richard and Clara Winston and Sr. Mary Frances McCarthy (San Francisco: Ignatius Press, 1997), pp. 31, 38, 42, 45; emphasis added.

6. All this means that, in taking up the Scripture for preaching, the preacher must first ask: How does this living Word revive, accentuate, or intensify my present, lived encounter with Jesus Christ? For if what the preacher preaches cannot be verified in his own experience, it is to that extent not "true". The hearers look for the correspondence between what the preacher proposes and the effects of the encounter apparent in the preacher's life. Then preaching becomes an event. The perception of that "something different" in the preacher is what makes all the difference for the hearers of the preaching.

7. Preaching as an encounter is eventful if the hearers are moved to use their freedom to adhere more closely and completely to Jesus Christ. The several effects of an encounter—wonder, newness, courage, insight, certainty, excitement, gladness, enthusiasm, etc.—become palpably evident in the hearers. What they hear and receive in the preaching corresponds to the needs of their hearts.

Conclusion

Let us give the last word of this chapter to the late, renowned Dominican theologian Father William J. Hill, with a quotation from his exceptional essay "What Is Preaching?"—in my judgment, one of the best treatises on the nature of preaching ever written:

> The preacher can be viewed as one who mediates a saving encounter of the believer with the living God. The locus of the encounter is the Word of God seen as his

utterance towards mankind, constituting his sovereign and saving initiatives towards men and women.... What should take [the preacher's] interest is ... [the Word's] character as God's offer and summons to men and women of today to respond in faith to his proffer of salvation.... The Scriptures themselves bring this about ... by initiating us into dialogue with their own subject matter ... which is God in his saving activity.[16]

With the incentive provided by Father Hill, we are ready to turn our attention to the locus of the preaching encounter: the Word of God.

---

[16] William J. Hill, O.P., "What Is Preaching? One Heuristic Model from Theology", in *A New Look at Preaching*, ed. John Burke (Wilmington: Michael Glazier, 1983), pp. 113, 116.

CHAPTER 3

The Soul of Preaching:

Piercing the Pearl of Sacred Scripture

"May the words of the Gospel wipe away our sins."

—THE ROMAN MISSAL

IN JANUARY OF 2007, Albert and Peter Kottke were hiking out of the Gila Wilderness in New Mexico as they finished an eight-day backpacking trip. While they were trekking, they heard a faint sound coming from the other side of the Gila River. Peering across the water, they saw a figure, hunched over and moving slowly—a figure that was . . . a woman. The brothers crossed the river and came upon Carolyn Dorn, a fifty-two-year-old camper who had been lost in the Gila National Forest for five weeks. The young men gave her food: almonds, dried apples, an energy bar, noodles, cheese—she had not eaten in three weeks. And she was too weak to walk out of the wilderness on her own; Albert and Peter would have to go for help. Would the woman be all right in the meantime? It was only when the brothers offered her a book—their copy of a suspense novel—that Carolyn's eyes lit up. With that, the brothers knew that the traumatized woman would be fine.

What Carolyn Dorn needed to stay alive was a word. Her eyes lit up, not at the food, but at a book. In this she represents every human soul. After his own forty-day sojourn in the wilderness, the famished Jesus told his tempter, "Man does not live by bread alone but by every Word that comes from the mouth of God." For there is a sustenance to God's Word, an efficacy—it is life-saving . . . the answer to our deepest hunger. Monsignor Lorenzo Albacete, in referring to the writings of Monsignor Luigi Giussani, says that the Word of God is that of which everything consists. Things exist because God speaks them. The Word of God is the consistency of all things. Father Maurice Zundel stresses this where he states:

> If you open the missal where the Church has gathered a few of the most beautiful texts of Scripture for your daily nourishment, your silent soul will soon experience the feeling of an ineffable encounter, and you will understand that the Bible is more than a book: it is a presence, a person. It is the eternal Word which greets you in every one of its words, the Word of the Father in whom is every Truth and who is Truth itself.[1]

By design, Sacred Scripture provokes a response in us at the level of the *I*, experience, and encounter. The renowned Scripture scholar Amos Wilder, in his must-read classic *Early Christian Rhetoric*, elaborates on this eloquently:

> One of the earliest and most important rhetorical forms in the Church was the story. This is theologically significant. The new movement of the Gospel was not to be identified with a new teaching or a new experience but with an action and therefore a history. The revelation was

[1] Maurice Zundel, *The Gospel Within* (Sherbrooke: Editions Paulines, 1993), p. 79.

in an historical drama.... The locus of the new faith was in concrete human relationships and encounters. Therefore the new community, living out a new kind of human and divine relationship naturally rehearsed models of Jesus' actions and interactions, since it was through these that the saving work of God had initiated its course.... Perhaps the special character of the stories in the New Testament lies in the fact that they are not told for themselves, that they are not only about other people, but that they are always about us. They locate us in the very midst of the great story and plot of all time and space, and therefore relate us to the great dramatist and storyteller, God himself.... The stories of the New Testament ... span our lives and wait our answer. To use a slang expression, they "put us on the spot." The stories are so graphic that we are bound hand and foot. Our consciences must stand and deliver. What is interesting here is the suggestion that it takes a good story to make people realize what the right thing to do is. The road to a moral judgment is by way of the imagination! One is tempted to say that aesthetics and ethics are not so far apart in the Gospel as is often supposed.... This new plain rhetoric of the Gospel was what it was only because it was prompted by a new direct speech or word of God himself to men. What makes such stories and such dialogue so formidable is that in each one God, as it were, forces us to give him a face-to-face answer.... The personal dramatic character of the Gospel itself necessarily involves confrontation, not instruction in the ordinary sense but the living encounter of heart and heart, voice and voice, and that this has inevitably registered itself in the ongoing story of the Christ and in the style of the New Testament. As we have observed, it is as though God says to men one by one: "Look me in the eye." [2]

[2] Amos N. Wilder, *Early Christian Rhetoric: The Language of the Gospel* (Cambridge, Mass.: Harvard University Press, 1971), pp. 68, 57, 60, 48, 54. (Amos Wilder was the brother of the famous playwright and novelist Thornton Wilder.)

The Venerable John Henry Newman understood that "if a preacher's subject only be some portion of the divine message, however elementary it may be, however trite, it will have a dignity such as to possess him, and a virtue to kindle him, and an influence to subdue and convert those to whom it goes forth from him." [3]

Besides, have you ever wondered why, in the Order of the Mass, the Liturgy of the Word comes before the Liturgy of the Eucharist? Could it be that that structural precedence reflects a priority integral to faith itself? After all, the Lord instituted the Eucharist as the Last Supper at the conclusion of his preaching ministry, not as a First Supper at the beginning of it. And, as the *Catechism* states, "the Lord Jesus inaugurated his Church by preaching the Good News" (*CCC*, no. 763, quoting *Lumen Gentium*, no. 5).

The point is this: Do we preachers have the same hope in the Word of God we preach that the starving Carol Dorn had in that novel? For, as the *Catechism* clearly teaches, liturgical preaching is not disconnected from the Word of God; rather, "the minister's homily . . . extends its proclamation" (*CCC*, no. 1154).

What Scripture Isn't

The Bible is not a textbook, an instruction manual, a rule-book, a chronicle, an annals, an almanac, a handbook of principles, a collection of sayings, a compendium of formulas, an enchiridion of verbatim quotations, an encyclopedia, or Cliffs Notes for salvation. If Sacred Scripture were a catechism or a code of canon law, then those publications would not otherwise exist . . . but they do.

[3] John Henry Newman, *The Idea of a University* (Notre Dame, Ind.: Notre Dame University Press, 1982), part 2, art. 6, p. 310.

In commenting on the nature of Sacred Scripture, Monsignor Luigi Giussani says that "we find ourselves with a document which, like others, is based upon *memory* and, in an original way, intends to make an *announcement*. The form of the document reflects its intention.... It seeks to trace the memory of an exceptional fact which someone, believing it was vital to tell others, transmitted." [4] To support his thesis, Giussani cites Rudolf Schnackenburg: "The evangelists had no intention of providing a shorthand record of what Christ said or a report of his actions such as a police officer might do." [5] This claim is substantiated, moreover, in Vatican II's Dogmatic Constitution on Divine Revelation, *Dei Verbum*:

> After the Ascension of the Lord, the Apostles handed on to their hearers what he had said and done. This they did with that clearer understanding which they enjoyed after they had been instructed by the glorious events of Christ's life and taught by the light of the Spirit of truth. The sacred authors wrote the four Gospels, selecting some things from the many which had been handed on by word of mouth or in writing, reducing some of them to a synthesis, explaining some things in view of the situation of their churches and preserving the form of proclamation but always in such fashion that they told us the honest truth about Jesus. For their intention in writing was that either from their own memory and recollections, or from the witness of those who "themselves from the beginning were eyewitnesses and ministers of the Word" we might know "the truth" concerning those matters about which we have been instructed (no. 19).

So then, what sort of book *is* the Bible? The Bible is a work of inspired *literature*; it is *art*. It is meant to be read with the

---

[4] Luigi Giussani, *At the Origin of the Christian Claim* (Montreal: McGill-Queen's University Press, 1998), pp. 37–38.

[5] Ibid., p. 36.

same kind of literary predisposition that we show to a novel, a poem, a letter, a short story, a play, or any other narrative. And unless Sacred Scripture is appreciated for its literary aesthetic, it cannot be interpreted or preached in an adequate way.

To make clear what I mean, I will rely extensively on the work of the late great Jesuit biblical scholar Father Luis Alonso Schökel. His book *The Inspired Word: Scripture in the Light of Language and Literature* is one of the most educative and exciting books on Scripture that I have ever read (and it is regrettably out of print). In *The Inspired Word*, Father Alonso Schökel explains: "The Scriptures are a reality of literary language. Their resources are abundant and their content full. They are an integrally human reality, and not simply a doctrinal textbook. They can contain all of revelation, but not in propositional form."[6]

Why does God purposefully employ a literary mode to mediate salvation to us via Sacred Scripture? Because

> a literary work presents to us new aspects of reality and experience.... The Scriptures often provide us with a knowledge born of familiarity; this is the way we come to know God as Someone Who comes and associates with men.... A work of literature reveals our own inner meaning and depth, and makes us conscious of ourselves. As we read, we see ourselves in the light of the author or of his work, and in virtue of this knowledge we can respond by acting to change ourselves.... This most important aspect of the truth of the Scriptures can never be adequately conveyed in propositional form.[7]

[6] Luis Alonso Schökel, *The Inspired Word: Scripture in the Light of Language and Literature* (New York: Herder and Herder, 1965), p. 161.

[7] Ibid., pp. 318, 147.

Tertullian agrees with this position:

> In order that we might have access to God more fully and
> more swiftly, in his determinations and designs he has added
> the means of literature to aid those who might wish to
> seek God, to find him whom they seek, and once found,
> believe in him, and believing serve him. . . . The words [of
> the prophets], and the miracles which they performed in
> order to lead men to faith in the divinity, are now kept in
> the treasury of literature where they are available to us even
> now.[8]

But would Scripture not be clearer, more exact and un-
ambiguous if the Bible instead had been written in a scientific idiom (like the *Catechism* or the *Code of Canon Law*)?
Alonso Schökel replies that "if the Scriptures had used a
technical language, they would undoubtedly be more precise, but they would not be so rich. . . . Scripture will always
contain more revelation than is formulated in dogmatic def-
initions."[9] This is why we have the *Acts* of the Apostles,
not the *Facts* of the Apostles.

Monsignor Lorenzo Albacete—who was trained as a phys-
icist—tells a story about his first meeting with his friend
Karol Wojtyła (before the latter became Pope John Paul II).
Wojtyła asked him, "What is the privileged language or
medium to communicate a human word? Is it your science?" Albacete replied, "No. Whenever I had girlfriends,
I didn't write to them in equations." Wojtyła said, "So what
is it you wrote to your girlfriends? It was poetry and drama;
it was symbolic thought." Because that alone communicates what is in the heart. Nothing else is able to embrace
the fullness of it. And that is why Sacred Scripture

---

[8] Tertullian, *Apologeticum*, 18; quoted in ibid., p. 125.
[9] Alonso Schökel, *Inspired Word*, pp. 168–69.

communicates by way of the language of symbolic thought as opposed to "scientific equations". (This is why fundamentalism is a deficient way to interpret the Bible.)

This expressly narrative dimension of Sacred Scripture ensures its inexhaustibility. Saint Ephraem the Syrian says: "Having acquired something rich ourselves, we do not suppose there can be nothing else in the Word of God besides what we ourselves have found. On the contrary, we realize we have only been able to discover one thing among many others. Having been enriched by the Word, we do not imagine the Word has been impoverished thereby; unable to exhaust its riches, we give thanks for its immensity." [10]

Father Hans Urs von Balthasar reinforces this:

> The idea that one has understood a passage of Scripture finally and completely, has drawn out all that God meant in it, is equivalent to denying that it is the Word of God and inspired by him.... Inspiration involves a permanent quality, in virtue of which the Holy Spirit as *auctor primarius* is always behind the word, always ready to lead to deeper levels of divine truth those who seek to understand his Word in the Spirit of the Church. [11]

Sacred Scripture does not simply relay ideas or transmit information, even in its revelation of doctrine. "We cannot lower the Word of God to the level of just one more theology manual.... [In the] integral language of the Bible, there is no such distinction between dogma and life, between theory and practice." [12]

---

[10] St. Ephraem the Syrian, *Commentary on the Diatessaron* 1.18–19; quoted in Raniero Cantalamessa, *The Mystery of God's Word* (Collegeville, Minn.: The Liturgical Press, 1994), p. 17.

[11] Hans Urs von Balthasar, *The Word Made Flesh*, vol. 1 of *Explorations in Theology* (San Francisco: Ignatius Press, 1989), p. 21.

[12] Alonso Schökel, *Inspired Word*, pp. 373, 148.

For the Scriptures, in particular the Gospels, are the re-presentation of God's unending saving *events* in the form of *word*. "Just as all the actions of Christ are words because they speak of the Father, so too all the words of Christ are actions and are endowed with power." [13] Father Francis Martin writes:

> Though the Gospel texts move on a less abstract level, the things that Jesus lived through and accomplished are nar-rated there because the events themselves continue to be revelation. It is the function of the narrating text to so configure the event that the "entropy" of the event may now function through contact with the "entropy" of the text. Because the events in the life of Christ, mediated to us through the Gospel narratives, are able to reveal him, they were called the "mysteries" of his life by later gen-erations who contemplated and experienced the open qual-ity of these events in their power to touch and change lives. [14]

Alonso Schökel echoes this: "God wishes to reveal Him-self to us as a Person, inviting us to friendship.... The mys-tery of Christ is articulated in a series of ordered events, which sum up salvation history.... To set forth the mean-ing of these events is to manifest their transcendent truth. This is fundamentally the truth of Scripture." [15]

And it is not "meaning" alone that Scripture manifests. Francis Martin makes a crucial distinction: "The testimony of the Scriptures makes not only meaning claims, but truth claims. It professes to portray the true perspective on reality,

---

[13] Ibid., p. 359.

[14] Francis Martin, *Sacred Scripture: The Disclosure of the Word* (Naples: Sapi-entia Press, 2006), pp. 50–51.

[15] Alonso Schökel, *Inspired Word*, p. 313.

and this in a way that is binding on all and not merely meaningful to some." [16]

Moreover, Alonso Schökel singles out another ramification of Scripture as Event-become-Word that we tend to overlook:

> When event becomes word, it is not merely repeated, but receives in the process a human and personal interpretation. To interpret is not to falsify; as a matter of fact, it is just the opposite. It means to penetrate into the meaning of an event and transpose superficial appearances to the level of intelligibility.... In the work, we come into contact with events as interpreted.... It is that which in the event made it salvation history and thus is deeply relevant to our lives.... As present in the work, and actualized in the liturgy, they are the events in which God acts now.[17]

The Efficacy of Sacred Scripture

Therefore, it is entirely true to say that the Word of God—and the preaching of that Word—saves us. The Church document entitled *The Priest and the Third Christian Millennium* stresses that "the revealed Word, made present and actualized 'in' and 'through' the Church, is an instrument through which Christ acts in us with his Spirit" (chap. 2, no. 1). Alonso Schökel continues:

> Sacred Scripture, because it is the inspired Word, contains the doctrine of salvation and it possesses the power of salvation.... Holy Scripture not only teaches us, it acts on us; it not only teaches us to act, it makes us act.... The Word of God is a bearer of grace; it works salvation.... This

[16] Martin, *Sacred Scripture*, p. 23.
[17] Alonso Schökel, *Inspired Word*, pp. 300, 301.

point is crucial: It is not simply that the inspired Word speaks about Christ; it is rather Christ who speaks, and "with authority"; the text of the Bible does not only speak about grace, it is itself an act of grace. The Word of God is not only a font of truth, it is also a source of life.[18]

Thus, "the Scriptures initiate us into a dialogue with their own subject matter which is God in his saving activity."[19] Archbishop Mariano Magrassi, in speaking about *lectio divina*, comments: "Since it constantly receives life from the indwelling Spirit, the Word contains in itself the power to save.... It is not only truth; it is power. It not only teaches; it is at work in us. It not only shows us models to imitate; it causes us to act."[20] We attest to this truth when, after proclaiming the Gospel, with a kiss we silently speak the words assigned to us to say: "May the words of the Gospel wipe away our sins."

Accordingly, Saint Thomas Aquinas identifies four chief effects of Sacred Scripture: "In the speculative order, to teach the truth and to refute error; in the practical order, to take from evil and to incite to good. Its ultimate effect is to bring people to perfection."[21]

The verification of these effects appears in a story from the nineteenth-century, anonymous Russian spiritual classic *The Way of the Pilgrim*:

One day I was sitting in the barracks deep in thought. A monk came in to beg alms for the church. Those who had

[18] Ibid., pp. 348, 350, 373.

[19] William J. Hill, O.P., "What Is Preaching? One Heuristic Model from Theology", in *A New Look at Preaching*, ed. John Burke (Wilmington, Del.: Michael Glazier, 1983), p. 116.

[20] Mariano Magrassi, O.S.B., *Praying the Bible: An Introduction to* Lectio Divina (Collegeville, Minn.: Liturgical Press, 1998), pp. 31, 32.

[21] St. Thomas Aquinas, *Commentary on 2 Timothy*, cited in Alonso Schökel, *Inspired Word*, p. 363.

money gave what they could. When he approached me he asked, "Why are you so downcast?" We started talking, and I told him the cause of my grief. The monk sympathized with my situation and said, "My brother was once in a similar position, and I will tell you how he was cured. His spiritual father gave him a copy of the Gospels and strongly urged him to read a chapter whenever he wanted to take a drink. If the desire for a drink did not leave him after he read one chapter he was encouraged to read another and if necessary still another. My brother followed this advice, and after some time he lost all desire for alcoholic beverages. It is now fifteen years since he has touched a drop of alcohol. Why don't you do the same, and you will discover how beneficial the reading of the Gospels can be. I have a copy at home and will gladly bring it to you." I wasn't very open to this idea so I objected, "How can your Gospels help when neither my efforts at self-control nor medical aid could keep me sober?" I spoke in this way because I never read the Gospels. "Give it a chance," continued the monk reassuringly, and you will find it very helpful." The next day he brought me his copy of the Gospels, I opened it, browsed through it, and said, "I will not take it, for I cannot understand it; I am not accustomed to reading Church Slavonic." The monk did not give up but continued to encourage me and explained that God's special power is present in the Gospel through his words. He went on, "At the beginning be concerned only with reading it diligently: understanding will come later. One holy man says that 'even when you don't understand the Word of God, the demons do, and they tremble.' " [22]

All of this confirms that "God's Word is living, and the inspired text is meant to come alive for us and awaken in us the same life that it awakened in its authors.... The Scriptures are true in the sense that they reveal to us what

[22] *The Way of the Pilgrim*, trans. Helen Bacovcin (Garden City, N.Y.: Doubleday, Image Books, 1978), pp. 30–31.

we are in the sight of God."[23] The "truth" of Sacred Scripture is the way it changes our lives, converting us and configuring us to Jesus Christ. As Saint Thomas Aquinas expresses it, "the Word of God is said to be a fire because it illuminates, it inflames, and it intimately penetrates, because it liquefies and it consumes the disobedient" (*In Jeremiam*, chap. 5).

How Does Scripture Mean?

How does this salvific effect take place in us? Father Francis Martin explains that the sacred words of Scripture create within us an inner capacity to receive the action of the Holy Spirit, who applies the saving events of Jesus Christ to our life right now. Jesus' saving events are offered to us now via the Word.

And the literary "allure" of the Bible remains an integral element in Scripture's faculty to create an inner capacity by which to receive the Spirit's saving actions. Since it is comprised of stories, we are drawn to read them. "The Bible was not written for biblical scholars, nor *Don Quixote* for Cervantists, nor *The Divine Comedy* for Danteans."[24] The Scriptures are written in the way that they are written so that people will pick them up, read them, and understand.

Again, this is why God, in his inestimable wisdom and providence, deliberately chose the mode of literature to be a medium of salvation. For "if God, in a personal exchange, wishes to reveal himself to us as a Person, then he must use the medium of language in all of its functions.... This most important aspect of the truth of the Scriptures [that

[23] Alonso Schökel, *Inspired Word*, pp. 113–14, 319.

[24] Luis Alonso Schökel, *A Manual of Hermeneutics* (Sheffield: Sheffield Academic Press, 1998), p. 170.

we come to know God as someone who comes and associates with people], can never be conveyed in propositional form."[25]

The Preacher's Approach to Scripture

When preaching falters, very often it is the result of the preacher not using an approach to Sacred Scripture adequate to the preaching event. When that happens, the preacher lacks what he needs to "mine" the riches of Scripture ... to harness the abundant potential of the sacred text—all that it has to offer in the way that it offers it. Frequently this occurs because the preacher does not "expect enough" of the text; he does not ask the kinds of questions of the text that the text begs him to ask of it. Too often he opens the Bible looking for some "ethical point" or "lofty idea" to extract and convert into a homily; but being Christian is not the result of an ethical choice or a lofty idea. That is why Sacred Scripture offers so much more—it offers us an encounter with a Person.

For example, Scripture scholarship in the Church would be lost without the breakthroughs afforded it by the historical-critical method. Father Francis Martin makes the point that "the historical critical approach to the Scriptures has brought an enormous and precious increase in our understanding of the horizontal dimension of the text and the events it narrates."[26] At the same time, however, the text also has a "vertical dimension", and it does not pertain to the scope of the historical-critical method to address that. And yet, any authentic preaching of a sacred text demands that the vertical dimension of the Scripture be addressed.

[25] Alonso Schökel, *Inspired Word*, pp. 137, 318.
[26] Martin, *Sacred Scripture*, p. 70.

This is why Pope John Paul II (as reported by George Weigel at a talk I heard) contended that "the historical-critical method has serious and grave limitations for breaking open Sacred Scripture for homiletic purposes." Thus, Francis Martin concludes his remark about the historical-critical method by saying that it has "been unable to link the Jesus reconstructed by history with the one who sums up in himself all history".[27]

Let me cite a few others who help us to understand the importance of this matter. First, Father Alonso Schökel:

> Some comprehension of the [sacred] text exists before its historical genesis is known. If we know beforehand the circumstances in which it came into being, so much the better; but this should not be exaggerated, as if historical-critical comprehension were the only way to comprehend, or the only scientific way.... The historical-critical method exerts itself to recover or reconstruct the specific historical conditions under which texts were produced, with the aim of understanding and explaining their meaning. It wishes to do so in a controllable, systematic and, thus, scientific way. However, it has some limits: the power of conditions is diverse according to the type of text; the historical process is not strictly linear; very often, the first thing is to comprehend the sense of a text, and the second is to seek a setting in which to fit it.... The task is to understand and explain the sense of the text, not to be content with identifying its causes, author, or influences.... Knowing all the data about a text is not yet to understand the text.[28]

Father Hans Urs von Balthasar makes this observation:

> The claim of Jesus that runs through all his words and deeds ... is a challenge to Jesus-historians to be less niggardly with

---

[27] Ibid.
[28] Alonso Schökel, *Manual of Hermeneutics*, pp. 44–45, 47, 170.

the range of meaning they allow the text. . . . The first pre-requisite for understanding is to accept what is given just as it offers itself. If certain excisions are practiced on the Gospel from the outset, the integrity of the phenomenon is lost and it has already become incomprehensible.[29]

Father Raniero Cantalamessa comments in a similar vein:

Many scholars expounding the Bible deliberately confine themselves to the historical-critical method. . . . The secularization of the sacred has nowhere revealed itself so acutely as in the secularization of the Sacred Scriptures. Yet to claim to understand Scripture exhaustively by studying it exclusively with the instrument of historical-philological analysis is like claiming to discover what the Eucharist is through a chemical analysis of the consecrated host. Historical-critical analysis, even when carried to the heights of perfection, only represents the first step in knowledge of the Bible, the step concerning the letter.[30]

The Pontifical Biblical Commission's 1993 document *The Interpretation of the Bible in the Church* also addresses this qsconcern: "The historical-critical method . . . restricts itself to a search for the meaning of the biblical text within the historical circumstances that gave rise to it and is not concerned with other possibilities of meaning which have been revealed at later stages of the biblical revelation of the Church" (I.A.4).

And, finally, Pope Benedict XVI, in his book *Jesus of Nazareth*, explains: "The historical-critical method . . . is . . . a fundamental dimension of exegesis, but it does not exhaust the interpretive task for someone who sees the biblical writ-ings as a single corpus of Holy Scripture inspired by God. . . .

---

[29] Hans Urs von Balthasar, *Seeing the Form*, vol. 1 of *The Glory of the Lord* (San Francisco: Ignatius Press, 1982), pp. 543, 467.

[30] Cantalamessa, *Mystery of God's Word*, p. 83.

"It is important ... to recognize the limits of the historical-critical method itself." [31] This echoes earlier comments he had made on the same topic:

> The historical-critical method ... contained hidden dangers along with its positive possibilities: the search for the original can lead to putting the word back into the past completely so that it is no longer taken in its actuality. It can result that only the human dimension of the word appears as real, while the genuine author, God, is removed from the reach of a method which was established for understanding human reality. [32]

Moreover, Pope Benedict XVI, with striking candor, warns us about what he refers to as "purely scientific exegesis":

> The fact is that scriptural exegesis can become a tool of the Antichrist.... The common practice today is to measure the Bible against the so-called modern worldview, whose fundamental dogma is that God cannot act in history—that everything to do with God is to be relegated to the domain of subjectivity. And so the Bible no longer speaks of God, the living God; no, now *we* alone speak and decide what God can do and what we will and should do. And the Antichrist, with an air of scholarly excellence, tells us that any exegesis that reads the Bible from the perspective of faith in the living God, in order to listen to what God has to say, is fundamentalism; he wants to convince us that only *his* kind of exegesis, the supposedly purely scientific kind, in which God says nothing and has nothing to say, is able to keep abreast of the times. [33]

---

[31] Pope Benedict XVI, *Jesus of Nazareth* (San Francisco: Ignatius Press, 2008), p. xvi.

[32] Joseph Cardinal Ratzinger, preface, *Interpretation of the Bible in the Church.*

[33] Pope Benedict XVI, *Jesus of Nazareth*, pp. 35–36.

This is why Pope Benedict calls for "new methodological insights that allow us to offer a properly theological interpretation of the Bible".[34]

Therefore, if something in addition to the historical-critical method is required for preaching in order to enable us to pierce the pearl of Sacred Scripture, as the rabbis of old would say, then what do we need exactly? Father Alonso Schökel paves the way to the answer we have already detected:

> Since [Scriptural] language is literary, it cannot be simply transposed to the level of technical language. It must retain its images, its symbols, and its concretization, which reveal and veil the mystery without rationalizing it (theology). . . . This language is literary and not merely intellectual. . . . This language comes before concepts, notions, and terms, and its meaning cannot be obtained by a systematic purification of its literary qualities (theology). Since this language is literary its interpretation cannot consist formally of a conceptual categorization and propositional presentation of its contents. We must proceed from the first, elementary understanding of the literary text to one that is deeper and more explicit, and thence to the content of the message. Since this language is literary, it confers on words a substantial value; it subsists in them and lives by means of them; it is not a disembodied set of ideas which lives and moves independently of the words which incarnate it.[35]

At the time of this writing [2007], the Synod on the Word of God in the Life and Mission of the Church, scheduled for October 5–26, 2008, has not yet taken place. However, the Lineamenta for that Synod has been published, and it states: "The Bible, the Book of God and man, has to be read with a correct blending of its historical-literal sense and

---

[34] Ibid., p. xxiii.
[35] Alonso Schökel, *Inspired Word*, p. 162.

its theological-spiritual sense. A proper exegesis of the text, therefore, must be based on the historical-critical method enriched by other approaches. This is the basis of interpreting Scripture" (I.15).

Thus, it becomes clear that it is not "legitimate to approach the Bible with the object of dismantling it piece by piece in order to construct a few thousand propositions each one of which would contain an article of faith".[36] For the literary character of the Bible is integral both to *the way* Scripture means and *to what* Scripture means (its content). But this does not impose a constriction on Sacred Scripture; quite the contrary. "Thus, to classify Scripture as a work of art is not to deny that it conveys meaning; it is rather to penetrate into the manner in which it intends to signify. . . . Since Christ is the ultimate revelation of God, any new knowledge of God must consist in penetrating ever deeper into the fullness which dwells in Him. . . . [Scripture's] literary 'modes' convey the highest truth." [37] Cardinal Ratzinger agrees with this assertion where he writes: "The beautiful is knowledge certainly, but, in a superior form, since it arouses man to the real greatness of the truth." [38]

Actualization

Rather than "dismantling" Sacred Scripture, the preacher seeks to *actualize* it as he takes up Scripture for preaching. What do we mean by *actualization*? Actualization is a way

[36] Alonso Schokel, *Inspired Word*, p. 137.

[37] Ibid., pp. 260, 314.

[38] Joseph Cardinal Ratzinger, "The Feeling of Things, the Contemplation of Beauty", Message to the Communion and Liberation Meeting at Rimini, Italy (August 2002); published as "Cardinal Ratzinger on the Contemplation of Beauty", *Zenit* (May 2, 2005): http://zenit.org/article-12907?l=english.

of doing theological reflection on the Scriptures so as "to reveal their significance for men and women of today, ... to apply their message to contemporary circumstances, and to express it in language adapted to the present time" and thereby "to go beyond the historical conditioning so as to determine the essential points of the message". Moreover,

> the meaning of a text can be fully grasped only as it is actualized in the lives of readers who appropriate it. . . . Exegesis is truly faithful to the proper intention of biblical texts when it goes not only to the heart of their formulation to find the reality of faith there expressed but also seeks to link this reality to the experience of faith in our present world. . . . [Then] there is created a new context, which brings out fresh possibilities of meaning that had lain hidden in the original context (*Interpretation of the Bible*, IV.A.1; II.A.1, 2; II.B.3).

We will not be surprised at the concrete direction given by *The Interpretation of the Bible in the Church* in applying its findings to the Church's pastoral ministry of preaching: "The presentation of the Gospels should be done in such a way as *to elicit an encounter with Christ*, who provides the key to the whole biblical revelation and communicates the call of God that summons each one to respond" (IV.C.3; emphasis added).

In order to bring about this encounter in the preaching of Sacred Scripture, the preacher turns to the invaluable assistance provided by literary criticism. "Since the language of Scripture is literary, it demands a literary interpretation, and yet every interpretation still leaves the text unexhausted.[39]

---

[39] Alonso Schökel, *Inspired Word*, p. 161. For an excellent analysis of the major differences between literary criticism and historical criticism, see Mark Allan Powell's *What Is Narrative Criticism?* (Minneapolis: Fortress Press, 1990), pp. 7–10.

Lectio Divina for Preaching

I would like to propose to the preacher a little method for doing *lectio divina* with the Scripture texts to be preached. Why is *lectio divina* needed if I, as a preacher, am going to appropriate and thereby actualize a sacred text for preaching? As Alonso Schökel explains it:

> The appropriation of a text means opening oneself to it, receiving it as a source of personal meditation.... I am not a neutral reader. I do not read the Bible as an archaeological curiosity or as a simple object of study. If I read it and want to understand it in depth, I must allow it to shape and mold me. It is a living text, and its communication of meaning exercises an influence on life. It not only communicates knowledge but is a live and vivifying force. Whoever reads it is invigorated by its force and gradually becomes a Christian.[40]

As the esteemed twentieth-century theologian Father Louis Bouyer understood it, *lectio divina* is personal reading of the Word of God during which we try to assimilate its substance—a reading in faith, in a spirit of prayer, believing in the real presence of God, who speaks to us in the sacred text, while the reader strives to be present in a spirit of obedience and total surrender to the divine promises and demands. *Lectio divina* done attentively ensures that "all our vital energies ... come into play: understanding and its ability to penetrate in order to 'read within'; the will and its capacity for commitment; the heart and its ability to react affectively; the imagination and its unlimited creative power in order to reconstruct events".[41]

---

[40] Alonso Schökel, *Manual of Hermeneutics*, pp. 92, 139.
[41] Magrassi, *Praying the Bible*, p. 92.

The key to our method of *lectio divina* is very simple but absolutely indispensable: the preacher is to approach Sacred Scripture as if encountering a person. For only if we treat Scripture the way we would a person do we avoid the temptation of reducing, misreading, or depreciating the Bible. The twelfth-century Cistercian mystic William of Saint Thierry reminds us that the Scriptures need to be read and understood in the same spirit in which they were created. In all Scripture, diligent reading is as far from superficial perusal as friendship is distinct from acquaintance with a stranger, or as affection given to a companion differs from a casual greeting.

As you begin to pray over the Scripture text, keep in mind this guiding principle: "The inspired text is objective, in that it reveals facts and events; it is personal, in that it shows us God as personal in the act of revealing himself; and it is dynamic, calling forth and making possible a response on the part of man." [42] In order to appropriate the richness and nuance of the Scripture before him, the preacher wants to plumb the depths of each of these three dynamics at work in the text: the *objective* dynamic, the *personal* dynamic, and the *response* dynamic.

Objective Dynamic. Begin with the *objective dynamic*. As you pray over the Gospel, discipline yourself to notice all the facts and details provided by the Evangelist: the time of the episode, the setting, the important circumstances, the specifics of the occasion, the order of events, any editorial details like names, ages, or character traits, information that seems significant—anything that lends specificity and concreteness to a passage. If these factors have been included

---

[42] Alonso Schökel, *Inspired Word*, p. 143.

in a pericope, there is a reason for it. That reason is crucial to your preaching.

So, to return to the text of the Samaritan woman at the well in the fourth chapter of John as an example, a close reading of the text would make me stop and take note of the following details provided by the objective dynamic of the text: Jesus is in Samaria; he stops in Sychar; he sits down at Jacob's well; the time is noon; a solitary Samaritan woman is at the well drawing water with her water jar; she has had five husbands; etc. Each of these details is rich in significance, and if I am sensitive and attentive to the text, then I cannot help but ask one of the most important and helpful questions in the actualization of Sacred Scripture: *Why* does the Evangelist include these details? *Why* does he recount this episode in this particular way? *Why* does he disclose these specific facts to us (and not others)? The more we ask "why" of the text in this way, the more the text opens itself up to us and reveals its levels of meaning (the spiritual sense). A preacher must use his imagination in approaching a Scriptural text; that means taking nothing for granted, being curious about every element, and being dogged in looking for the reasons behind the choices made by an author in composing a text.

Father Alonso Schökel says:

A text is an answer to a question authors have asked themselves. . . . In interpretation, it is vital to know what we are asking a text. . . . The richness of a person who interprets a text (the exegete) lies in the plurality, quality, and variety of the questions formulated to the text. . . . What has been written with imagination must be read with imagination. The imagination is an extraordinary necessary organ of comprehension and interpretation.[43]

---

[43] Alonso Schökel, *Manual of Hermeneutics*, pp. 83–84, 85, 86, 90.

Therefore, the next step would be to do some research on these details: What is the historical and theological significance of Sychar ... of Jacob's well ... of the relationship between the Samaritans and the Jews in the days of Jesus? Why is the woman there at the well at the absolutely hottest time of the day? Here the assistance of the historical-critical method is invaluable in helping us get to the bottom of things. Make notes of your findings.

Personal Dynamic. Next, give your attention to the *personal dynamic*. God reveals himself through the persons and relationships that fill Scripture. To do this, first of all, take notice of the *dramatis personae*, the particular characters in a given episode. Who is named and who remains nameless? For this passage, the cast is Jesus, the Samaritan woman, the woman's would-be husband (who is not present but certainly prominent in the dramatic action), the disciples (when they return), and the Samaritans from town.

Secondly, make a little record of all the actions that transpire in the passage, especially the dialogue. Be especially attentive to the specific verbs used (in their original Greek, if you can). This can be a little tedious, but its payoff is great. For example, as noted before, there is a definite progression in the way that the woman speaks to Jesus: she first uses no title in addressing him, she calls him "Jew", "Sir" (Lord), "Prophet", until finally she leaves proclaiming him to be "Messiah". Jesus calls her "Woman". Jesus also exposes the woman's scandalous sins: "You have had five husbands, and the man you are living with now is not your husband."

Once you have compiled the raw data of the personal dynamic, then engage in a theological reflection of it. What does the progression of titles represent in terms of the woman's own spiritual progression? Who else in the Gospel of John does Jesus call "Woman", and what, therefore, is the significance of that term? What possible reason could Jesus have for exposing the woman's profligacy; how is this not a cruel thing to do? And is there any significance to the fact that Jesus, according to what the text indicates, is the seventh man? We could go on and on in our close reading and analysis of the text in this manner.

Response Dynamic. The third dynamic, the *response dynamic*, is the most subtle and, often, the most fertile for actualization. The document *Fulfilled in Your Hearing* makes an indispensable assertion about preaching: "The homily is not so much *on* the Scriptures as *from* and *through* them" (section III). To clarify, the steps to the response dynamic are the following:

1. Be very attentive to the syntax. What is distinctive about the sacred writer's vocabulary and lexicon? What special or conspicuous terms does he use? List any adjectives, adverbs, or other striking parts of speech. Wonder about word usage, turns of phrases.

2. With the aid of a good concordance like *A Modern Concordance to the New Testament* edited by Michael Darton, or *A Greek-English Lexicon of the New Testament and Other Early Christian Literature* edited by Walter Bauer and Frederick William Danker, study how the sacred author used the distinctive vocabulary or terms in the passage under consideration in the rest of the biblical book (and other books he wrote). After studying the composite use of a particular word, make a theological judgment about the

significance and implications of the sacred writer's use
of the term.

3. Pay special attention to any questions that are asked;
    they are almost always meant for us.

4. What images, repetitions, symbols, parallelisms,
    themes, or motifs are in the passage? Be very atten-
    tive to the sacred writer's style and "voice" as an
    author. What literary devices, techniques, proce-
    dures, and forms does he employ? For example, in
    chapters 18 and 19 of the Gospel of John (Christ's
    trial before Pilate), the scene alternates between the
    interior of the praetorium and the exterior where the
    crowd is assembled. John the Evangelist tells us very
    explicitly that Pilate came out to them (18:29); Pilate
    went back into the praetorium (18:33); Pilate went
    out again to the Jews (18:38); Pilate went out a sec-
    ond time (19:4); Pilate went back into the praeto-
    rium (19:9); etc. Obviously, if Pilate wants to speak
    to the people outside he has to "go out to them".
    Why does John take such pains to give us stage direc-
    tions that are really self-evident? Well, think about
    this for a moment: What if someone were acting the
    very same way with your refrigerator door? What
    would your response be? "Let's go! Make up your
    mind!" And that is exactly the point. John uses a lit-
    erary device—the narrative reenactment of Pilate's
    physical transitions in and out—to symbolize his inte-
    rior *vacillation and irresoluteness toward Christ* in a way
    that no degree of description or other means of expla-
    nation could approximate. The narrative form enables
    us to experience Pilate's vacillation personally.

5. What is the "subtext" of the passage—that is, what is implied but not explicitly stated? What can you read between the lines? What does the writer leave unsaid that carries a big impact on what the text is talking about (its "reference")? Read the Scripture as you would a detective novel, being especially attentive to any "clues" the author has inserted that will enable you to get at the heart of the mystery.

6. How does the text make you feel? What does it stir up in you emotionally, intellectually, spiritually? What does it make you think about? What does it make you conscious of? How do you relate to the text? How does the text "act" on you? What dilemmas does it raise? How does it provoke you? As literature, what new aspects of reality and experience does it awaken in you? How does it incite insight?

7. Take note of the context of this passage within the whole of the biblical book—how it factors in the book's structure. What comes before it and what comes after it? What does the placement of the passage in the book signify? How does it compare with other passages or books of the Bible; for example, in the case of the Gospels, are there parallel accounts of the same event?

8. What is the relationship of this passage with the entire Bible?

9. Once you have identified all the "evidence" and "clues" in the text, ask: *Why* are they there? What literary and therefore theological purpose do they

serve? Why is the story told the way it is? Be attentive to the intentionality demonstrated by the author. Look at everything. Examine everything. Consider everything. No "detail" is coincidental or insignificant.

10. Then ask: What does this Scripture reveal about Jesus Christ and, therefore, about me? What does this Scripture passage concretely propose? What's in it for me?

11. Prayerfully reflect on all you have considered.

12. Now you are ready to prepare your homily, for this work constitutes true *contemplare et contemplata aliis tradere*—to contemplate and to hand on to others the fruit of contemplation.

Apply this method of the response dynamic to the passage about the woman at the well. A predominating motif in the episode of the woman at the well is that of thirst. What does the passage mean by thirst? How is Johannine irony at work in this passage? What is the relationship between this passage and Christ's words on the cross: "I thirst" (Jn 19:28)? What is the significance of the questions that the woman asks? What is the "spring of water welling up to eternal life" (Jn 4:14)? What is a "prophet"? What was happening to the woman interiorly as she dialogued with Jesus? Notice that the episode is presented in the form of a little one-act play. Where else does this dramatic form appear in the Gospel of John? How do you react when you hear Jesus divulge to the woman her own sins? Why did he do it? Why does the woman respond so positively to Jesus? Why does the woman leave her water jar behind; what is the significance of that? Why would the townspeople—who presumably shunned the woman and considered her word worthless—believe the woman and go out to meet Jesus? And these are only a few of the questions that the text begs us to ask of it. But notice that we have not yet consulted a commentary. Simply plumbing the literary depth of the text has yielded so much richness.

Saint Gregory the Great promises that the divine words grow with one who reads them. Where the mind of the reader is directed, there, too, the sacred text ascends; for ... it grows with us, it rises with us. When we manage to get this close to the sacred text through our diligent *lectio divina*, then we become personally aware that "the text breathes" (Paul Claudel).

Conclusion

Saint Gregory the Great, in one of his letters, offers the best of invitations: "Come to know the heart of God in the words of God." And Lacordaire urges us: "Keep reading the Holy Scriptures over and over again. With the Bible and the *Summa* of St. Thomas Aquinas, one can attain anything." [44]

[44] Henri-Dominíque Lacordaire, *Letters to Young Men* (London: Art and Book Company, 1902), p. 95.

CHAPTER 4

Putting the Word into Words:

The Language of Preaching

"The mystery of language brings us back to the inscrutable mystery of God himself."

—POPE JOHN PAUL II

D ID YOU HEAR THAT?" Nothing terrifies us like an unexpected, unidentified sound. Even if we *see* nothing, the fact that we *heard* something upsets the status quo, puts us on alert, maybe makes us anxious. We know there's something *there*. All on account of a little noise. Why? Because sound signifies. When the prophet Elijah—holed up in a cave evading murderous enemies—heard "a still small voice", he hid his face in his cloak and went and stood at the entrance of the cave ... because he recognized that the Lord was in that tiny sound (1 Kings 19:12–13).

Sound and Presence

Before concept, before word, preaching is first and simply ... sound. There are three astounding things about sound. I learned these from the writings of the late great Jesuit scholar Father Walter Ong. Consideration of these dynamics of sound makes our appreciation of preaching more "sound".

There is a correlation between sound and presence. Sound, as it were, puts us in the middle of things; it makes us feel "immersed". Think about listening to a symphony orchestra—it is as if the music envelops us; it creates a world that we can enter. We love "surround sound" precisely because of the semblance of presence, of immediacy and incorporation that it creates. There is something especially "existential" about sound that is not as true of the other senses. Father Ong writes: "Through sound we can become present to a totality which is a fullness, a plenitude.... Sound and hearing have a special relationship to our sense of presence. When we speak of a presence in its fullest sense ... we speak of something that surrounds us, in which we are situated. 'I am *in* his presence,' we say, not 'in front of his presence.' " [1]

Sound expresses interiority. According to Father Ong, "sound has to do with interiors as such, which means with interiors as manifesting themselves.... Sound reveals interiors.... The sound of a violin is determined ... by the shape of the interior cavity in the body of the violin, and other interior conditions." [2]

Sound generates a sense of mystery. Hence our very visceral reaction when surprised by a sound we were not anticipating. The production of a sound bespeaks the presence of a something or a someone. Once perceived, it evokes our attention, our concern, our wonder. Saint

---

[1] Walter J. Ong, *The Presence of the Word: Some Prolegomena for Cultural and Religious History* (New York: Simon and Schuster, 1970), p. 130; New Haven: Yale University Press, 1967.

[2] Ibid., pp. 117, 118.

Thomas Aquinas was of the opinion that people are more persuaded by what they hear than by what they see. There is always something behind a sound. The dynamic of sound takes our attention off ourselves and prompts us to look beyond, to listen, to await.

The ramifications of all this for preaching quickly become apparent.

"Let Me Hear Your Voice"

If it is true that sound reveals what is interior about a thing, we can understand very well why so many individuals are afraid of speaking in front of other people. For men, *voice* is the paradigm of all sound. We get intimidated by the prospect of public speaking precisely because we sense that if we speak out loud in front of others we will expose our interior self; we will stand before others spiritually naked. Comedian Jerry Seinfeld comments on the findings of a recent survey about people's greatest phobias. The poll shows that the top fear now is that of public speaking—a finding that surpasses the previously highest-ranked fear: the fear of death. This leads Seinfeld to quip that nowadays people at a funeral are more fearful about giving the eulogy than showing up in the casket.

Thus, the act of using our voice, of speaking, is an act of great power. In fact, it is synonymous with who we are as "persons". The derivation of the word "person" itself implies the exercise of voice: *per* and *sonare*—"to sound through". In a certain respect, *we are* our voice—we cannot conceive of a voice apart from the person to whom it belongs.

Sound generates a sense of presence and mystery; the sound that is voice reveals a person to us *and* provides the preeminent way for persons to be united with one another. Pope John Paul II explains that "a human person establishes contact with all other entities precisely through the inner self.... It is true that a human person's contact with the world begins on the 'natural' and sensual plane, but it is given the form proper to man only in the sphere of his interior life."[3] How, then, are we able to establish contact with other persons through the inner self? By way of speech. "To address or communicate with other persons", notes Father Ong, "is to participate in their inwardness as well as in our own.... Encounter between man and man is achieved largely through voice."[4]

To substantiate this, Father Ong offers a fascinating example: the situation of two people standing face to face with their eyes locked on each other. "Looking fixedly at another person has normally the effect of reducing him to a surface, a non-interior, and thus to the status of a thing, a mere object. One can, however, look at another without limit of time so long as a conversation is going on. Speech establishes the specifically human relation that takes the edge off the cruelty of vision."[5] Amazing! What otherwise would be construed as a dehumanizing, antagonistic act—rude staring—becomes, through the mystery of voice and speech, transformed into friendly beholding—a conversation that theoretically could go on forever.

This happens because, as Father Ong says, "voice is not inhabited by presence as by something added: it simply conveys presence as nothing else does.... Even the voice of one dead, played from a recording, envelops us with this

[3] Karol Wojtyła, *Love and Responsibility* (New York: Farrar, Straus and Giroux, 1981), p. 23.

[4] Ong, *Presence of the Word*, p. 125.

[5] Ibid., p. 166.

presence as no picture can."[6] This helps us to understand
in a new way why Jesus the Good Shepherd asserts again
and again that it is the *voice* of the Shepherd that leads and
guides his sheep (Jn 10:3, 4, 5, 16): because the Shepherd
wants to impart to his sheep, not just direction or protec-
tion, but his very Presence. "Voice ... is the manifestation
of presence, and as such has permanent religious possibilities."[7] Especially for preaching.

We Need a Good Talking To

If a Benedictine monk does something gravely wrong, the
Rule of Saint Benedict specifies a particularly effective punishment, namely, "excommunication". But this is intended
literally: the monk is to be out of communication with the
others in the monastery "until by due satisfaction he
obtaineth pardon". Chapter 24 of the Rule stipulates that
a guilty brother is not "to intone a psalm or antiphon in
the oratory, nor read a lesson." Chapter 25 adds: "Let none
of the brethren join his company or speak to him.... And
let him not be blessed by anyone passing by." What makes
this punishment so effective is that, while the offender
remains in the midst of the community, he is forbidden to
speak and others are prohibited from speaking to him.
Experience shows that nothing reforms an errant monk as
does such shunning. The imposed muteness constitutes a
kind of fasting that increases a person's desire for real companionship. Community deprived of communication is hell.

We wither without effective communication. Communication closes the distance between us. We communicate
with words and language so as to become more fully

[6] Ibid., pp. 114, 101.
[7] Ibid., p. 168.

ourselves. "Sight", says Father Ong, "may provide a great deal of the material to think *about*, but the terms *in* which all people do their thinking corresponds to words." [8] Helen Keller was reluctant to refer to "wordless sensation" as "thought". The philosopher Monsignor Robert Sokolowski makes the point that "all experience involves some ... articulation, and if the experience is at all complex, it involves language." [9]

The efficacy of word and language upon us is greater and more far-reaching than we may realize. In 2006, a neuroscientist named Adrian Owen conducted an experiment on a vegetative patient to see if such patients could perform a complex mental task on command. He asked a woman who had been severely injured in a car accident (but who was able to hear and understand), to picture herself playing tennis—forehand, backhand, etc. To the neuroscientist's astonishment, the "vegetative" woman's response registered on a brain scan was indistinguishable from those of a group of normal volunteers. Another example: the finding of a recent study on stuttering reveals that people with this speech impediment are able to speak freely when they do so in unison, for example, when a group recites the Pledge of Allegiance. Somehow the speaking-with-others enables them to overcome whatever impedes their ability to speak on their own. Communication does this.

Words carry power: "Words, which can make our terrors bravely clear, / Can also thus domesticate a fear" (Richard Wilbur). [10] It is this awareness of the efficacy of words

[8] Ibid., p. 14.

[9] Robert Sokolowski, *The God of Faith and Reason: Foundation of Christian Theology* (Washington, D.C.: The Catholic University Press, 1995), p. 135.

[10] Richard Wilbur, "A Barred Owl", in *Mayflies: New Poems and Translations* (New York: Houghton Mifflin Harcourt Publishing, 2000).

that stops us from talking about worms at table when people are eating spaghetti. A report by the American Academy of Orthopedic Surgeons states that during periods of great stress in patients, physicians' words that seem immaterial or are uttered in jest might become fixed in the patient's mind and cause untold harm. Elie Wiesel once remarked, "Be careful with words—they're dangerous. Be wary of them. They beget either demons or angels." Why is this? As Louis Lavelle understands it:

> It is because words disclose our thought, and, once uttered, have given it a form, that they begin to bind us.... A word, once spoken, suffices to change the state of things, but without appearing to do so. It upsets the relationship between two persons, even when it does not bring to light anything which they did not already know; the point is precisely that it brings it into that light. What was once merely a latent possibility, still in suspense, has now come into the open. What existed only in my soul has emerged without. No one can avoid taking it into account, and henceforward the whole of my conduct is conditioned by it.[11]

Communication does this.

One day a few years ago a seventeen-year-old boy in a deep coma was admitted to the hospital. With one look the neurosurgeon on duty announced, "He won't live until morning—and it's a good thing, because he'd be a vegetable." Thankfully, a seasoned and savvy nurse, Nancy Valko, judged otherwise. In her thirty-year career, Valko demonstrated an uncanny ability to bring comatose patients out of their comas. Her methods were simple: she talked to the patients, played their favorite music, made simple

---

[11] Louis Lavelle, *The Dilemma of Narcissus* (Burdett: Larson Publications, 1993), pp. 86–87.

requests of them. In fact, the seventeen-year-old did live through the night. And before long, he was even able to make small movements when the nurses asked him to. Strangely, though, the boy would not respond when the neurosurgeon was in his room. Eventually the boy recovered to such a degree that he was discharged from the hospital and sent home. Time passed until one day a handsome young man walked into Valko's ward and asked, "Do you remember me?" The once-comatose boy had returned to say thank you. When Valko mentioned the neurosurgeon, the young man replied, "I remember him calling me a vegetable. I wouldn't move for him." Communication does this.

The Helen Keller Phenomenon: A Paradigm

Perhaps the most famous example of the liberating, life-giving power of voice, word, language, and communication is the story of Helen Keller ... as she herself tells it. Three months before Helen Keller was seven years old, her teacher Anne Sullivan had tried to teach the blind and deaf girl language by using a porcelain doll, which Keller promptly smashed on the ground. In her autobiography, Keller confesses to being "keenly delighted when I felt the fragments of the broken doll at my feet. Neither sorrow nor regret followed my passionate outburst. . . . In the still, dark world in which I lived there was no strong sentiment or tenderness." She then continues to relate what happened that day:

> We walked down the path to the well-house. Someone was drawing water and my teacher placed my hand under the spout. As the cool stream gushed over one hand

she spelled into the other the word *water*, first slowly, then rapidly. I stood still, my whole attention fixed upon the motions of her fingers. Suddenly I felt a misty consciousness as of something forgotten—a thrill of returning thought; and somehow the mystery of language was revealed to me. I knew then that "w-a-t-e-r" meant the wonderful cool something that was flowing over my hand. That living word awakened my soul, gave it light, hope, joy, set it free! There were barriers still, it is true, but barriers that could in time be swept away. I left the wellhouse eager to learn. Everything had a name, and each name gave birth to a new thought. As we returned to the house every object which I touched seemed to quiver with life. That was because I saw everything with the strange, new sight that had come to me.[12]

Take note of all the remarkable things that happen once "the mystery of language" is revealed to Helen Keller. Her first response to the experience of verbal communication is not to acknowledge her comprehension of a new idea, her intellectual grasp of some concept. Rather, the revelation of the significance of the word "water" *restores to her her "I"!* Helen Keller erupts in a kind of confession speaking in language that is resurrectional: "That living word awakened my soul, gave it light, hope, joy, set it free! . . . I left . . . eager to learn. . . . Everything . . . seemed to quiver with life. . . . I saw everything with the strange, new sight." This is the miracle of correspondence—Keller's dormant heart recognized in the grasp of that word what it had been waiting for forever. In summing up the meaning of the event at the well-house, Helen Keller attests to the most transformative effects of an encounter. More than just a way of "understanding", Helen Keller was given a new and condign way to make sense of reality. Though still physically

---

[12] Helen Keller, *The Story of My Life* (New York: Bantam, 1990), p. 16.

blind, *she could see* with "strange, new sight". In short, she had been given an awareness of Mystery. But without the event of communication offered to her by Anne Sullivan, Helen Keller would have remained lost in her still, dark, wretched, and unremorseful world.

As a teacher, Anne Sullivan was a genius. Helen Keller's deafness excluded her from the experience of sound. Yet Anne Sullivan realized that nonetheless she needed to break through Helen Keller's "still, dark world" devoid of sentiment and tenderness. To do so, she would need to find a substitute "voice", that is, an alternate means by which to reach Keller's interior self to engage in a true encounter with her ... to penetrate her constricted world so as to introduce her to a greater one ... to generate in her a sorely lacking sense of mystery. Literally, the word became "sound" through her flesh—the flesh of her fingers in contact with the flesh of little Helen's hand.

The role of preaching is to be that event of communication for those who do not live at the level of their *I* and who, therefore, languish for light, hope, joy, freedom, new life, new sight, the rebirth of reason. And they may not even *know* that they are languishing until a preacher takes them by the hand and presses the Word Become Flesh into their flesh, lifting the misty consciousness of something forgotten so as to let in the Presence of the One they have been waiting for all their lives. The sacred communication of preaching can do this.

And even more ... for the story of the miracle of that dialogue-event at the well does not end there. Remember the porcelain doll that Helen Keller meanly smashed "with neither sorrow nor regret" and in whose broken fragments she "keenly delighted"? It, too, played a role in the encounter that brought about Helen Keller's awakening:

On entering the door I remembered the doll I had broken. I felt my way to the earth and picked up the pieces.
I tried vainly to put them together. Then my eyes filled
with tears; for I realized what I had done, and for the first
time I felt repentance and sorrow. I learned a great many
new words. I do not remember what they all were; but I
do know that *mother, father, sister, teacher* were among them—
words that were to make the world blossom for me, "like
Aaron's rod, with flowers." It would have been difficult to
find a happier child than I was as I lay in my crib at the
close of that eventful day and lived over the joys it had
brought me, and for the first time longed for a new day
to come.[13]

Again, a close reading of what Helen Keller went to great
pains to remember and recount yields up marvels. Thanks
to the encounter that happened in Keller through the event
of communication, she was transformed even *morally!* She
wanted to make reparation—literally—for her wrong-doing
(attempting to piece the broken doll back together). The
awakening of her *I* imbues her, for the first time in her
life, with a sensitive conscience, a sense of sin, and with
remorse: "For the first time in my life I felt repentance
and sorrow." No mere discourse can bring this about in
a person; this is the fruit of communication that is an
encounter. Moreover, with her *I* wide open and with energized reason and wonder, Helen Keller in that same day
"learned a great many words". And while she admits,
"I do not remember what they all were", look at the
words *she does* remember: *mother, father, sister, teacher*. All
of these are words that refer to *relationships!* Clearly, she
remembers these new words of this new day because these
relationships were integral to the encounter that would

[13] Ibid., pp. 16–17.

remain with her the rest of her life. The closer she stayed to the persons in these relationships, the more that encounter would give her life a new horizon. The event of the communication encounter on "that eventful day" filled her with a joy that made her long for every new day to come.

Thanks to the encounter that Helen Keller called "my soul's sudden awakening", she became electrified with the meaningfulness of life, which she then began to pursue with an unstoppable passion. She writes: "The more I handled things and learned their names and uses, the more joyous and confident grew my sense of kinship with the rest of the world." Who can live without such kinship? Anne Sullivan gave Helen Keller a new language that was her "salvation"—that is, an escape from her own inability. Preaching is a language that saves us.

Why Preaching Is *Viva Voce*

When the Word became flesh, the Father did not send an *inscribed* Word—rather the Word was *spoken*. The utterance of God's Word called preaching continues this Event of the Incarnation.

In terms of preaching's meaningfulness, even before one considers the content of a homily or a sermon, the very fact that the preacher speaks to us—and the particular way in which he speaks to us—is deeply significant. Cardinal Danielou insisted that "preaching is not a discourse on God; it is the Word of God. It is an act of God working through the ministry of the priest. The Word of God for the Bible is not the mere enunciation of a thought. It contains a *dynamis*, an efficacy. . . . It touches hearts and converts them, it arouses faith, it brings about sanctification. It is alive.

Nothing can imprison it." [14] The medium of preaching—
the fact that it is a certain kind of speech—itself plays an
integral role in this faith arousing and sanctifying.

Amos Wilder points out a principal and perpetually relevant fact about the earliest Christian speech including that
of Jesus Christ himself:

> It is naïve, it is not studied; it is *extempore* and directed to
> the occasion, it is not calculated to serve some future hour.
> This utterance is dynamic, actual, immediate, reckless of
> posterity; not coded for catechists or repeaters.... *Viva voce*
> communication is more malleable, more personal and more
> searching. These qualities were to distinguish Christian
> discourse even when it was obliged to take on written
> form.... Jesus' speech had the character not of instruc-
> tion and ideas but of compelling imagination, of spell, of
> mythical shock and transformation. Not just in aesthetic
> sense but in the service of the Gospel. [15]

If Christ opted for the medium of such lively, personal,
immediate speech with which to encounter his hearers—
purposefully eschewing a medium that was didactic, academic, or pedantic—shouldn't every preacher of Christ do
the same? There was nothing *formalistic* about the manner
of speaking of Jesus Christ. Formalism, in my judgment, is
one of the foremost enemies of preaching today because it
is so abstract, so jejune, so unengaging at the level of the
I, so deadening—so boring. In a way, it doesn't matter *what*
the preacher has to say if the *way* he says it disregards my
heart, my experience, my *I*. A thing is received according
to the mode of the receiver. Deliberately and by design,

---

[14] Jean Daniélou, S.J., *Christ and Us*, trans. Walter Roberts (New York: Sheed
and Ward, 1961), pp. 180–81.

[15] Amos N. Wilder, *Early Christian Rhetoric: The Language of the Gospel* (Cambridge: Harvard University Press, 1971), pp. 12–13, 84.

Christ preached in a mode guaranteed to reach his receivers (hence the genius of the parables), for communication is not what is said but what is heard. I have no desire to listen to a preacher if preaching is not an encounter ... and the invitation to the encounter begins *in the very way that the preacher speaks.*

Christ chose a conversational mode for his preaching, not because it makes for more aesthetic oratory, but because it most faithfully adheres to the anthropological realities of authentic communication and the needs of the human *I*. Anyone engaged in genuine communication consents to act as a *mediator*. Louis Lavelle explains this:

> When two persons enter into communication ... what they transmit is nothing but the power to acquire, each through the other, what neither yet possesses. ... My aim is neither to awaken in you a state of mind which you already know all too well and which would take all heart out of you, because it would bring you back too sharply to yourself; nor, on the other hand, do I wish to awaken in you some state of mind as yet unknown to you, and which could bring you nothing more than some fleeting emotion. Genuine communication takes place only when each of the two persons is a mediator to the other, when each reveals to the other the deep, unknown desire he bears in the secret places of his heart; the discovery of another's solitude allows him both to break out of his, and to plumb its depths.[16]

To the woman at the well, Jesus reveals the deep desire of his thirst—a desire that he will proclaim in his cry from the cross ("I thirst!")—and the woman's desire for an authentic relationship in her life. He plumbs the depths of her solitude, thereby enabling her to break out of it. Christ's communication mediates to her the power to acquire the

---

[16] Lavelle, *Dilemma of Narcissus*, p. 55.

Possession that will change her life forever and stay with her forever.

It is true that Christ's intention in preaching was to persuade people to the Truth. But the Lord did not resort to the rules of debate or clever salesmanship to accomplish this. Christ's method of persuasion was not distinct from the method of the Incarnation. Lavelle writes:

> Influence on someone else is only possible on condition that one is not trying to influence him. Your desire to win me over to your point of view puts me on my guard, and stimulates opposition in me. Your thought is debased and corrupted, you are no longer single-minded, when you are thinking of your coming victory. A man influences another solely by what he is, not by what he is trying to do. The desire to insinuate himself into another mind in order to subject it to his own can only be prompted by [self-love], and this in turn is to corrupt the purity of his spiritual insight.[17]

Without question, Christ desires to convert the woman at the well from her adulterous ways and to win her over to the point of view of the Gospel. Jesus influences the woman to the point of utter personal transformation solely *by who he is*—by an encounter with his Presence. The woman says, "I know there is a Messiah coming." And Jesus responds, "I *who speak to you* am he" (the added emphasis is to highlight how Christ's identity is revealed in his act of speaking).

Furthermore, only communication that proceeds from who-the-speaker-is (vs. what he has to say) can effect authentic *dialogue*—the ultimate goal of all communication. Maurice Zundel says that "life's most illuminating dialogues (between a mother and her child, between a real

[17] Ibid., p. 163.

teacher and his pupils, ... between very close spouses, between faithful friends) are all effective because of the light that, rising from their depths, shines from one being to the other, and reveals to them the Presence in whom they are united. Words and concepts are internalized: ... they become *someone* when they are energized by the current flowing from soul to soul." [18] Cardinal Ratzinger comments on the same phenomenon:

> Dialogue first comes into being where there is not only speech but also listening. Moreover, such listening must be the medium of an encounter; this encounter is the condition of an inner contact which leads to mutual comprehension. Reciprocal understanding, finally, deepens and transforms the being of the interlocutors.... To listen means to know and to acknowledge another and to allow him to step into the realm of one's own "I".... Thus, after the act of listening, I am another man.... When we speak of dialogue in the proper sense, what we mean is an utterance wherein something of being itself, indeed, the person himself, becomes speech. [19]

Perhaps what is most moving about Christ's dialogue encounter with the Samaritan woman at the well is the dramatic way that Jesus, by listening to the woman to the point of effectively hearing her confession, enables the woman to "step into the realm of her own *I*", to become another, new woman. She proclaims: "Come, see a man *who told me* all that I ever did!" She professes that it is Christ's speaking/listening—and the self-revelation it has brought about—that converts her; she has been given no catechism lesson.

[18] Maurice Zundel, *The Inner Person, Finding God Within* (Sherbrooke: Médiaspaul, 1996), pp. 86–87.

[19] Joseph Cardinal Ratzinger, *The Nature and Mission of Theology*, trans. Adrian Walker (San Francisco: Ignatius Press, 1995), pp. 32–33, 34.

Lavelle describes the same dynamic in this way: "Communication with another person can only take place in a domain which is above them both, and as the result of an impulse through which each of the two, forgetful of self, and thinking only of the other with intent to help him to reach a higher plane, receive from him forthwith the very life which he is seeking to bestow." [20] When the disciples return to the place of the well and are surprised to see Jesus "talking with a woman", curiously, "none said, ... 'Why are you talking with her?'" Could it be because even they sensed a communication that was taking place in a domain above them all?

All of this makes perfect sense for, as Josef Pieper showed us in chapter 2, belief is the result of assenting to a trusted *someone* who proposes something to our freedom. Monsignor Giussani expands on this insight:

> An individual lives the experience of a deeper conviction when he finds himself adhering to the message of another rather than when he sees for himself. In adhering to someone he is listening to, man, in fact, must rest the *totality* of his person on the "you" of another. And, while it is very easy for all of us to doubt ourselves, it is much harder to cast the shadow of our "ifs" and our "buts" on a presence we admire and love. In any person-to-person relationship, the totality of our "I" is put into play so that knowledge and love form a oneness, and the act of adherence to the truth concerns the *totality* of the factors constituting life.... The Lord... so as to facilitate the bond between man and truth (which is Himself) chose as his instrument not the terms of a vision, but those of an abandonment, of a love, the process by which man follows the testimony of truth.... A child grows through the

testimony of this mother and father as they continually propose solid ground for him to walk on.[21]

Gospel preaching exists to be the means for people to attain this "deeper conviction" that comes, not through self-reliance, but through adhering to another. It is not the "message" of the other that commands our attention but the "you" of the other. If the preacher is an admirable and lovable presence, we find it nearly impossible to resist or contradict what he proposes. We abandon ourselves to the love that moves the preacher to approach us in the first place. Like little children, we listen and accede to the testimony of the preacher whose motivation of love toward us assures us that whatever he proposes is solid ground for us to walk on. "The true motive of communication is affection." [22]

When it's all said and done, communication ultimately is not about conveying ideas, transmitting new information, or imparting knowledge. As Ratzinger once observed, conversation between people only comes into its own when they are no longer trying to express something, but *to express themselves*, when dialogue becomes communication.[23] The dialogue known as preaching becomes true communication when the preacher expresses himself as that self is revealed in his living, irresistible relationship with Jesus Christ. Then, as John Henry Newman assures us, preachers "may with practice attain such fluency in expressing their thoughts as will enable them to convey and manifest to their audience that earnestness and devotion to their object, which is the life of preaching—which both covers,

---

[21] Luigi Giussani, *Why the Church?* (Montreal: McGill-Queen's University Press, 2001), pp. 80, 81.

[22] Luigi Giussani, *The Risk of Education* (New York: Crossroad, 2001), p. 111.

[23] Joseph Cardinal Ratzinger, *Introduction to Christianity* (San Francisco: Ignatius Press, 2004), p. 95.

in the preacher's own consciousness, the sense of his own deficiencies, and makes up for them over and over again in the judgment of his hearers." [24]

When all this happens, then preaching stands the chance of being sublime in the sense that the third-century Greek rhetorician Longinus understood it. Longinus says that if something is sublime, "it makes it difficult or impossible for the hearer to resist its appeal, it leaves the hearer with more food for reflection in the hearer's mind than the mere words convey, it remains firmly and ineffaceably in the memory, and it touches the hearer with a sense of grandeur." Sublime communication can do all this because it is an event that begins from the experience of the hearers, engaging them at the level of their *I*, offering not mere ideas but a presence that brings about an encounter which reawakens in them the religious sense. As Longinus put it, "the effect of sublimity upon an audience is not persuasion but transport" for "sublimity is the echo of a great soul." [25] Preaching becomes sublime when the preacher lets his great soul resound. As Cardinal Ratzinger sums it up, "Every great human utterance reaches beyond what was consciously said into greater, more profound depths; there is always, hidden in what is said, a surplus of what is not said, which lets the words grow with the passing of time." [26]

The Implications for Preaching

We have said a lot about sound, voice, word, language, communication, and speech. Let us put it together

---

[24] John Henry Newman, *The Idea of a University* (Notre Dame: Notre Dame University Press, 1982), part 2, art. 6.7, p. 321.

[25] Longinus, *On the Sublime*, 9.2.

[26] Joseph Cardinal Ratzinger, *Truth and Tolerance: Christian Belief and World Religions*, trans. Henry Taylor (San Francisco: Ignatius Press, 2004), pp. 254–55.

in order to see how it helps us make better sense of our preaching:

1. Too often preachers make the mistake of approaching preaching from the perspective of the mechanics of public speaking. Misplacing the priority of preaching makes for a defective conception of it. The point of this chapter has been to show what communication is and how even the rhetorical elements of preaching are ordered to the ontology of the *I*. Saint Thomas Aquinas warns that preachers preoccupied with rhetoric "do not intend to lead people to an admiration for what they say, but only for the way they say it." [27]

2. The encounter that preaching brings about begins with the preacher's voice. The preacher's voice has the power to make the hearer aware of a presence, to reach into the interiority of the hearer so as to speak to his deepest self, and to generate a sense of presence and Mystery. The medium of the preacher is speech that is lively, conversational, down-to-earth, direct, immediate, personal—*not* formalistic. The preacher's voice can be deeply soothing and consoling; it can be a powerful instrument that prompts people to follow Christ.

3. Communication has consequences. A stray or thoughtless word can debilitate. Conversely, communication carried out in communion can rehabilitate. The experience of being deprived of communication confirms just how much the possibility of our flourishing as human beings is dependent upon the communication

[27] St. Thomas Aquinas, *Contra Impugnantes Dei Cultum et Religionem*, 12.

we engage in each day. Preachers need to be attentive to these dynamics of communication.

4. The example of Helen Keller reinforces how much the revelation of a word can bring about an awakening of the soul. The preacher's task is to find new and compelling language capable of breaking through the spiritual blindness and deafness that imprison so many people.

5. The preacher serves as a mediator. The influence that a preacher exercises on his hearers is the result of the revelation of *who he is*—one set apart by God to proclaim the Word of God. A preacher can be such a mediator only if he is a person deeply convicted by the Gospel and his love for Jesus Christ. So many of the problems that arise concerning preaching require the help, not of a public-speaking tutor, but of an able spiritual director or a friend in the faith.

6. The true motive of all communication to the well-desposed is affection. The conversation of preaching becomes a true dialogue when the preacher intends to express, not simply a spiritual idea or a doctrinal position, but rather to express his lived encounter with Jesus Christ. People are willing to listen to preaching because they are looking for a worthy some "one" to follow. The bond that flows from such communication is what brings about deeper conviction in believers.

7. When the preacher is obedient to these properties of communication, the likely outcome is that his preaching will be sublime. The preacher becomes an

attractive person—a great soul—whose preaching is irresistible. His hearers are left not only with a lot to think about but with a new *way* of thinking. What the preacher proposes becomes an unforgettable good in the hearers' lives; in this sense, preaching is "memory"—an event that keeps happening. People want to return to hear such a preacher again and again. For what the preacher brings about is not just "persuasion" but "transport". The preacher reawakens and reignites the religious sense in his hearers, giving them a sense of grandeur . . . a sight of Mystery . . . the hope for their own destiny.

Conclusion

The nineteenth-century German theologian Johann A. Mohler, in speaking about the Lord, expressed the excruciating dilemma of every human heart: "I don't think I could go on living if I stopped hearing Him speak." The proof of it is what we beg for just before receiving Holy Communion: "Lord, . . . only say the word and I shall be healed." People hear Christ speaking through the speech of our preaching. May our utterance of God's holy Word truly be a healing word.

CHAPTER 5

Homiletic Missteps:

The Poison of Moralism and Its Antidote

"You have to meet love before meeting morality. Otherwise it's torture."

—ALBERT CAMUS

TO UNDERSTAND WHY moralism doesn't work you simply have to drive south down the Major Deegan Expressway toward New York City. Take Exit 3: the Grand Concourse/E. 138th Street. When you come to the intersection at the end of the ramp, you'll notice that the extreme right lane is reserved for RIGHT TURNS ONLY. You will know this because that traffic law is painted in huge white letters on the asphalt in front of your car. It is also posted on impossible-to-miss signs placed on the side of the road. And in case you overlooked all that, it is also plastered on a placard suspended over the intersection. But here's the thing: *every single time* that I have driven through that intersection (i.e., often), someone gets in that right lane but ends up going straight; the driver does not turn right. This demonstrates that something more is necessary than simply telling people what the rules are in order to get them to do what is right (and in this case, to *take* a right).

What Is Moralism?

What do we mean by "moralism"? It all goes back to that
first paragraph of *Deus Caritas Est*. Being Christian is *not*
the result of an ethical choice. Moralism, however, posits
exactly that. Moralism presupposes that if a person com-
plies with a predetermined moral formula, then fulfillment
and human flourishing will follow. That is, moralism presumes that happiness is the result of moral initiatives. It contends that merely heeding the rules, the precepts, the laws,
the dogmas, the commandments of Christianity will make
someone a good Christian. But all of that results only in
"right doing". And being Christian is not first and foremost about "what we do". Being Christian is about *who we
are*. Being Christian is the result of the encounter with an
Event, a Person—with Jesus Christ in the flesh. Moralism
is a bastardization of the faith because it leads to mere *behavior* and not to a *Person*.

To this extent, moralism remains a legalistic way of approaching morality since it sets out to reduce life's worth
to ethics or ideology—to an abstraction. Moralism would
have us evaluate life according to the standard of a preconceived code of behavior. Thus, moralism is a kind of idolatry because it equates the meaning of life with the mere
keeping of God's laws instead of friendship with him.
Accordingly, moralism caters to the sway of original sin in
us by which we contrive to manage and measure reality
according to standards that we ourselves comprehend and
control.

The insidiousness of moralism is the flagrant inadequacy
of its proposal: it proposes a *plan* and not a *Person*. "Moralism is the reduction of the mystery of the faith to a list
of dos and don'ts" (J. M. Sullivan, O.P.). Moralism deludes

us into thinking that God is more desirous of our moral irreproachability than he is of our union with him in Jesus. The root of Christ's complaint about the scribes and Pharisees is their abominable moralism. "Woe to you lawyers also! for you load men with burdens hard to bear, and you yourselves do not touch the burdens with one of your fingers" (Lk 11:46).

In practice, moralism enforces moral obligations on people without specifying how the good proposed corresponds to their elementary experience—the needs of their hearts. Lacking this, the moral instruction comes across as unreasonable . . . no matter how "right" it objectively may be. To moralize is to enjoin a moral ideal on others without *explicitly* indicating how grace is the means for effecting it . . . without *explicitly* clarifying how the initiative of God enables the faithful to do what otherwise to them appears impossible . . . without *explicitly* revealing how the given course of action is integral to the realization of human happiness.

The renowned Dominican moral theologian Father Servais Pinckaers writes:

> The advent of faith effects an original and substantial transformation in the moral life. It centers the moral life on a particular person: Jesus, the Christ. In his historical particularity—in his body that suffered and was resurrected—Jesus becomes the source and cause of justice and wisdom. In short, he becomes the source and cause of moral excellence for those who believe in him. Jesus is not merely a sage or a model. By means of the personal ties that faith and love initiate, he establishes such a close spiritual communion between himself and his disciples that St. Paul will present the Christian life as "life in Christ." He even affirms that, "It is no longer I who live, but Christ who lives in me" (Gal 2:20). This view is unique among

the moralities and religions of the world: For Christians, the person of Jesus has become the center of the moral life.[1]

Look at Saint Peter's preaching in chapter two of the Acts of the Apostles. The sermon is brilliant in its simplicity and completeness; all Peter does basically is remind the people of *what happened* . . . of the Events of Christ that took place in their midst so that, faced with them anew, they might use their freedom to make a judgment about them. And because Peter's preaching is a compelling encounter, the people are "cut to the heart" when they hear all he has to say (see Acts 2:37). So much so, that the people then beg Peter and the other apostles, "What shall we do?" (Acts 2:37). That is, they *expressly ask* for moral direction. Do you think that the people would have responded to Peter in that way if he had begun his preaching with a long list of moral injunctions? Of course not; they would have turned and headed in the opposite direction. But instead, the people come to the leaders of the Church begging for insight and guidance.

This New Testament episode confirms an essential dynamic of the human condition: "Reason, once it realizes that God is the source of everything, that the Mystery lies at the origin of everything, is also keen to discover the paths that lead on to the moral laws, the paths that lead on to how we should treat God, how to behave towards God. In other words, reason, once it becomes aware of what God is, of the fact that he is, is keen to discover the itineraries of human behavior."[2]

[1] Servais Pinckaers, *Morality: The Catholic View* (South Bend, Ind.: St. Augustine's Press, 2001), pp. 86–87.

[2] Luigi Giussani, quoted in Communion and Liberation, *You or About Friendship: Exercises of the Fraternity of Communion and Liberation* (Rimini, 1997), p. 51.

Much of moralism, I'm guessing, is well-intentioned: the motive being to motivate people to live in an ethically upright way. The trouble is that moralism begins from a mistaken and—what's worse—demeaning view of the human *I*. For moralism is predicated on the Socratic fallacy that holds that if people are simply informed of the difference between right and wrong they will do good and avoid evil. But a reading of Romans 7:14–25 (about Saint Paul's dilemma with sin) shows the problem with that theory.

Moreover, there is something obtuse about moralism. Who among us likes to be ordered around and told what to do? Louis Lavelle comments: "Man always rebels against a law imposed on him from without; instinctively he doubts its validity, and suspects that somebody's interest is present in disguise. He seeks to act in the full light of knowledge, and desires that knowledge should be sufficient to motivate his acts." [3] But "the full light of knowledge" is immaterial for moralism. Jean Vanier further describes this dynamic as it applies to correcting another person:

> If you have to reprimand someone and say, "You have done this, admit it;" if you only show the law and nonconformity to the law, you will find that no man can accept his sin, no man. He will either find excuses or he'll go away despairing. You must not reveal to people their sin, their poverty, without at the same time showing them that they are loved and that there is hope; that they can do better. If you show only the law, you crush, bringing despair and revolt. But if through all your attitudes you show how much you hope and believe in this person, then, and then only, can you show him what was not right. [4]

[3] Louis Lavelle, *The Dilemma of Narcissus* (Burdett: Larson Publications, 1993), p. 208.

[4] Jean Vanier, *Followers of Jesus* (Guelph: Alive Press Ltd., 1973), p. 89.

But moralism is morality conceived merely as a calculation of principles that impinge on human action and that judge it abstractly. It is not the ambit of moralism to elucidate why these principles are right or wrong—why people should or should not comply with them. In this deficient mentality, moralism bases its authority for what it demands on statements like, "because the Bible says so", or "because that's what the Church teaches". And, as Vanier insists, that is not a sufficient incentive to move people to listen or to accede. The mere pronouncement of laws or doctrines—no matter how worthy—cannot impel a person's freedom to adhere to the good. Men simply aren't made that way. "Human beings are not converted by having truths about Jesus presented to them but by having Jesus himself presented to them." [5]

Moralism is an attempt to convert people to rectitude according to an *ought* instead of according to an *attraction*. In the process, moralism disdains human freedom and degrades the faith. As Pope John Paul II warned, "the temptation always remains of understanding the revealed truths of faith in purely functional terms. This leads only to an approach which is inadequate, reductive, and superficial at the level of speculation" (*Fides et Ratio*, no. 97). Like few other scourges facing the Church, moralism reduces the faith to such functional terms.

At the same time, moralism spawns a pernicious form of self-reliance. Then–Cardinal Ratzinger addressed this threat:

> The temptation to turn Christianity into a kind of moralism and to concentrate everything on man's moral action has always been great. For, man sees himself above all. God

[5] Raniero Cantalamessa, *The Mystery of God's Word* (Collegeville, Minn.: The Liturgical Press, 1994), p. 43.

remains invisible, untouchable and, therefore, man takes his support mainly from his own action. But if God does not act, if God is not a true agent in history who also enters into my personal life, then what does redemption mean? Of what value is our relationship with Christ and, thus, with the Trinitarian God? I think the temptation to reduce Christianity to the level of a type of moralism is very great indeed even in our own day.... For we are all living in an atmosphere of deism. Our notion of natural laws does not facilitate us in believing in any action of God in our world. It seems that there is no room for God himself to act in human history and in my life. And so we have the idea of God who can no longer enter into this cosmos, made and closed against him. What is left? Our action. And we are the ones who must transform the world. We are the ones who must generate redemption. We are the ones who must create the better world, a new world. And if that is how one thinks, then Christianity is dead.[6]

The rich young man of the Gospels is the archetypal proponent of moralism. He presumes that his impeccable record of commandment-keeping makes him a shoo-in candidate to be the Lord's disciple. But Christ requires something of him that clearly has never crossed the man's mind, obsessed as he is in his own indubitable duteousness. Jesus tells the man to sell everything. By that gesture of radical dispossession, the man is put in the position to begin his life from a new perspective. Up to this point, he has viewed his life as a program to complete instead of as a relationship to live. The rich young man must be disabused of his moralistic way of assessing accomplishment, of reckoning "virtue". That is the new chance that Jesus Christ offers the man when he says to him, "Follow me." The pathetic thing

[6] Joseph Cardinal Ratzinger, "The Power and the Grace", *30 Days*, no. 10 (1998): 31–32.

is that the rich young man *leaves Jesus Christ*. He is more attached to his moralistic sense of self-esteem, more interested in being commended and promoted for his success in keeping moral laws than he is in having a relationship with Jesus Christ. The man leaves Christ's presence preferring his own ideology over the Word Made Flesh and the infinite possibilities for happiness offered in his Person.

More than ten times in the fifteenth chapter of John, Jesus Christ spends the night before his death pleading/commanding: "Remain in me." Why this uncharacteristic reiteration? Jesus purposefully includes this plea among his last words because he knows how prone we are to the lure of moralism. He realizes our inclination to seize on some "formula" that promises to exonerate our shame, validate a questionable way of life, rationalize compromised moral choices, etc., instead of living our vocation, which is *union with Jesus Christ*. "'And I, when I am lifted up from the earth, will draw all men to myself.' Into this union with Christ all men are called" (*CCC*, no. 542, quoting *Lumen Gentium*, no. 3).

The Poison of Moralism

The contrivance of moralism divorces the *teaching* of Christ from the *Person* of Christ, undoing the Incarnation by turning Jesus Christ into an idea. Cardinal Carlo Caffarra once remarked that "the dirtiest trick that has been played on modern man has been to make him believe that the doctrine and morality taught by Christ were worth more than his person, and that, after all, we could even do without him."[7] However, this derelict tendency goes all the way

[7] Quoted in Andrea Tornielli, "Inversion of Method", *Traces* 4, no. 1 (2002): 30–31.

back to the day of Saint Augustine, who recognized it and emphatically repudiated it: "This is the horrendous and hidden poison of your error: that you claim to make the grace of Christ consist in his example and not in the gift of his Person." [8]

Such a proclivity reveals that the real problem lies in how we understand reality.

> Jesus judges his generation not on the basis of its level of ethical blamelessness, but on the way it approaches reality.... We are always concerned with ethics. The problem is not one of ethics but of ontology, our relationship with reality. Because if I have a desire for infinity in my heart, I cannot find the answer myself; I have to accept Someone Else, I have to let Someone Else come in. And if I am impenetrable, I cannot let Someone Else in, and this is my damnation. Hell is this: this ultimate impenetrability.[9]

This "impenetrability" is the root of all immorality; it is the cause of despair. And unless a proposal of morality connects me to the Someone who can satisfy my desire for infinity, then the demands of morality only exacerbate the despair that haunts me. The only fitting proffer of morality is the one that overcomes my resistance to let that Someone in. For Christ is not looking for our ethical blamelessness but our willing openness. Conversely, moralism, because of the way it entrenches me in my own individualism, defiance, and self-righteous self-reliance, only reinforces the personal hell I have claimed for myself.

[8] St. Augustine, *Contra Iulianum opus imperfectum*, II, 146.

[9] Fr. Julián Carrón, quoted in Communion and Liberation, *Event of Freedom: Exercises of the Fraternity of Communion and Liberation* (Rimini, 2003), p. 26; and in Communion and Liberation, *You Live for Love of Something Happening Now: Exercises of Fraternity of Communion and Liberation* (Rimini, 2006), p. 44.

At a talk I was giving for a group of well-educated, well-to-do, lay Catholics, one man became openly indignant when I pointed out the evil of moralism; he acted as if I had defamed something sacred . . . as if I had violated his rights. But moralism is the violation, . . . and it begins with how we look at reality.

Berating people with moral "oughts" only antagonizes them, aggravating their impenetrability. Moralism at best produces only guilt-inducing conformism and not liberating obedience. Obedience is the way that I overcome my false self in my heart. Authentic morality is about letting Someone in.

The Marks of Moralism

How do I know if my preaching is moralizing? There are a number of typical, predictable forms that moralistic preaching takes.

One basic form of moralistic preaching might be termed *diagnostic*. This is preaching quick to point out whatever is wrong—preaching "bad news". It addresses the ills that afflict God's people without administering Christ's cure. Another form is *voluntarism*. This is preaching that overrates the potential of the unaided will to attain moral perfection. Voluntarism equates sanctification with an intensification of will power. It directs people to "imitate" the saints without giving them any indication how such imitation is possible for weak, sinful souls. It is usually expressed in exhortations that amount to "Just try harder." A third variation of moralism is *ultimatum* preaching—preaching centered on the shibboleth "Do this/don't do that, or else" as a (defective) means of persuasion. Ultimatum preaching seeks to capitalize on servile

fear ("hellfire and brimstone" preaching). All of this under-
scores how inappropriate it is for preaching to ask the question "What am I to do" before first addressing the question
"Who am I?"

The predicament regarding so much moralistic preaching is that, if we didn't know better, we would think we
were actually doing people a favor. We say to ourselves:
People need to know the difference between right and
wrong, right? Not to mention the fact that moralistic
preaching is *the easiest* preaching imaginable. How hard is
it to stand up in front of people and spout decrees, dispense admonishments, or point an accusatory finger ... all
the while remaining conveniently detached and feeling
superior?

Hans Urs von Balthasar singles out a more sinister—
and disturbing—reason for the proliferation of moralism in
preaching, namely, doubt:

> Most preachers keep to abstractions because, in the final
> analysis, they are afraid that one of their listeners will
> actually take something concrete seriously and put it into
> practice, here and now. Rhetoric is the compensation for
> the fact that the absolute does not appear possible. The
> preacher knows in advance, as it were, that he is a useless
> servant, and, in order at least to appear to be useful, he
> does "everything"—everything that can be done in this
> way. And this same sense of despair is also the source of
> the endless stream of moralizing that flows from the
> pulpit.[10]

The only way out of the tyranny of moralism is through
the appropriation of genuine morality.

---

[10] Hans Urs von Balthasar, *The Grain of Wheat: Aphorisms* (San Francisco: Ignatius Press, 1995), p. 118.

What Is Authentic Morality?

My activated religious sense tells me that the meaning of
my life lies outside of me in the Mystery who made me.
This is also the starting point of authentic morality: for if
to be myself I have to begin by looking beyond myself—to
the relationship that I am with the Infinite—then the same
holds true of morality. Morality must begin with something greater than myself.

To be "moral", then, is to "remain in the original attitude God gave you by creating you.... You are open to the
real." [11] Put another way, "morality ... is the mind's original openness, an original attitude of availability and dependence." [12] The moral person recognizes that the reason for
his existence lies in an Other, and the most reasonable way,
then, to live one's life is by relying on that Other. Morality, thus, means maintaining an attitude of attentiveness
toward that Other: God. "Morality is impoverished when
it is divorced from mystery." [13]

In this way, Gospel morality is not acquiescence, not *cohe-
sion* to a preconceived code. As Father Pinckaers explains:

> Catholic moral teaching is not a mere code of prescrip-
> tions and prohibitions. It is not something that the Church
> teaches merely to keep people obedient, doing violence
> to their freedom. Rather, Catholic morality is a response
> to the aspirations of the human heart for truth and good-
> ness. As such, it offers guidelines that when followed make
> these aspirations grow and become strong under the warm
> light of the Gospel. Catholic morality is not by nature

[11] Luigi Giussani, *The Religious Sense* (Montreal: McGill-Queen's University
Press, 1997), p. 123.

[12] Carrón, quoted in *Event of Freedom*, p. 26.

[13] Mariano Magrassi, O.S.B., *Praying the Bible: An Introduction to* Lectio Divina (Collegeville, Minn.: Liturgical Press, 1998), p. 96.

oppressive; nor is it in principle conservative. It seeks to educate for growth. This is its true mission.[14]

Morality, then, is a *tension* . . . attention toward reality. Monsignor Giussani writes: "To say that morality is a state of tension means that we are in a position that is continually directed toward something that is Other. It means that we stand open to correction, so that we may enter more easily into a reality that is higher than we are. Our satisfaction lies in affirming God and reaching out to him."[15]

Thus, morality is a relationship with reality that springs from the acknowledgment of a Presence in my life that is the answer to my life. "Morality is born as a prevalent, irresistible liking for a person who is present: Jesus. . . . Man's morality is born, then, as friendship with God as Mystery and therefore with Jesus. Therefore, morality for a Christian is loving adherence."[16] It is not a coincidence that Christ's preaching begins with these words *in this order*: "The time is fulfilled and the kingdom of God is at hand; repent, and believe in the gospel" (Mk 1:15). The all-captivating Presence of Jesus Christ in our midst is what makes us want to repent; the possibility of that repentance becomes apparent through Christ's Presence. Morality means giving in to this Presence. If being Christian is the result of an encounter with a Person, then Christian morality itself must be an encounter with this Person.

The paradigm for Gospel morality is Peter's Yes. At the moment when the risen Jesus appears to him, Peter is a scandalously immoral man: he has capitulated to cowardice, he has deserted Jesus Christ, and he has publicly denied

---

[14] Pinckaers, *Morality*, pp. 1, 2.

[15] Luigi Giussani, *The Risk of Education* (New York: Crossroad, 2001), p. 36.

[16] Giussani, quoted in *You or About Friendship*, pp. 31–32.

knowing him. And yet, to "convert" Peter, the Lord simply asks him a question: "Do you love me?" In response,
Peter does not enumerate his egregious sins; he does not
remind Christ of the enormity of his evil. Before the compulsion of Christ's question, Peter is not tempted to wal-
low in his misdeeds and guilt. Why? Because something
even greater than the sum total of his iniquity has taken
hold of him, has enabled him to live his *I* again, has provoked him with a hope that wrenches him out of the
wretchedness of his sin. And that "something" is his
morality—the winning attraction of Christ's Presence.
Morality begins from the fact that no matter what our conscience accuses us of, no matter how viciously we have
violated the Law, in the Presence of Christ we cannot say
anything except, "Yes, I love you; I am with you; I belong
to you." This is ultimately the only "real" reality.

Our personal experience of the Presence of Christ makes
us "moral" because it moves us to conceive of the whole
of life through that adherence. Every choice and decision we make is the fruit of that adherence. There is nothing "extraneous" about our moral choice-making. Morality
flows from our friendship with Jesus Christ ... our Yes
to him. We *want* to follow every rule, precept, law,
dogma, and commandment of the Church—every "dot
of the law" (Lk 16:17)—because our Yes to the winning
attraction of Christ's love shows us the reason for such
obedience, makes us love the good of those mandates, and
endows us with an ability that we could never have outside of our union with Christ. The *Catechism* says that
by "revealing himself God wishes to make [men] capable
of responding to him, and of knowing him, and of loving
him *far beyond their own natural capacity*" (*CCC*, no. 52;
emphasis added).

In the light of Peter's Yes, we have the correct frame of mind for understanding well Cardinal Ratzinger's point regarding "moral obligation":

> Moral obligation is not man's prison, from which he must liberate himself in order finally to be able to do what he wants. It is moral obligation that constitutes his dignity, and he does not become more free if he discards it: on the contrary, he takes a step backward, to the level of a machine, of a mere thing. If there is no longer any obligation to which he can and must respond in freedom, then there is no longer any realm of freedom at all. The recognition of morality is the real substance of human dignity; but one cannot recognize this without simultaneously experiencing it as an obligation of freedom. Morality is not man's prison but rather the divine element in him. . . . The morality that the Church teaches is not some special burden for Christians: it is the defense of man against the attempt to abolish him.[17]

The travesty of moralism moves us to say Yes merely to a *law*. The "patron saint" of moralism is the Pharisee in the temple who, with unconscionable *philautia*, prays, "O God, I thank you that I am not like the rest of humanity—greedy, dishonest, adulterous" (Lk 18:11). It is plainly evident that the Pharisee's moralism has to a certain degree "abolished" his humanity. On the other hand, authentic morality moves us to say Yes to a *Love*; this is what the sinful tax collector in that same temple did. As a result of that Yes, our whole life is conceived through an adherence to a Person—not an ethic. We adhere so that we may please the face of the Presence. As a result, "every action—as relationship with God, with Jesus, with the humanity of the individual

---

[17] Joseph Cardinal Ratzinger, *A Turning Point for Europe?* trans. Brian McNeil, C.R.V. (San Francisco: Ignatius Press, 1994), pp. 36, 38–39.

and of society—is friendship. Every human relationship is
either friendship or otherwise it lacks something, it is defective or false." [18]

> Morality for the Christian is religion; and religion is love;
> and love is not a negative but a creative thing. . . . We must
> make sure that we are learning to see and love the law of
> God in terms of the life of God, and the clear-cut defini-
> tions and directives of ethics in terms of the freedom of the
> sons of God. Our Lord came primarily not to bring us an
> ethical code, but to bring us life. [19]

All the same, we must give moral instruction to our people in our preaching. So what do we do?

The Antidote for Moralism

We want our people to possess an understanding of Gospel morality that moves them to embrace that morality as
their way of life. A moralistic method sabotages that possibility. Saint Louis de Montfort recognized a moralistic tendency at work in preachers of his own time. As he put it,
"Many priests want to preach thunderously against the worst
kinds of sin at the very outset, failing to realize that before
a sick person is given bitter medicine, he needs to be pre-
pared by being put into the right frame of mind really to
benefit by it." [20]

There is a deliberate anti-moralistic rationale evident in
the very structuring of the *Catechism of the Catholic Church*.

---

[18] Giussani, quoted in *You or About Friendship*, pp. 51–52.

[19] Gerald Vann, O.P., *The Divine Pity: A Study in the Social Implications of the
Beatitudes* (New York: Scepter, 2007), pp. 43, 46–47.

[20] St. Louis Marie de Montfort, *Secret of the Rosary*, in *God Alone: The Collected Writings of St. Louis Marie de Montfort* (Bayshore, N.Y.: Montfort Publications, 1995), p. 160.

Notice where the treatment of the Ten Commandments is located. It is not in the first section of the *Catechism*, which is about who God is and the profession of faith. It is not in the second section, which is entitled "The Celebration of the Christian Mystery". This means that teaching people about the Catholic faith doesn't begin with the Ten Commandments. It is only after we have been introduced to the fact of God and to the indispensable role of the sacraments in knowing God that the Church proceeds to propose her moral teaching in the *third* section of the *Catechism*. To propose moral teaching according to any other order results in disorder.

Papal preacher Father Raniero Cantalamessa recognizes an identical intention in the way that Saint Paul structures his Letter to the Romans:

> The most important teaching in the letter to the Romans lies in its actual structure and arrangement. The Apostle does not first deal with Christian duties—charity, humility, obedience, purity, service—and then with grace, almost as if grace were the reward for duty well accomplished. On the contrary, he first deals with justification and grace and then with the duties that spring from these and which are made possible by grace.[21]

However, even a preacher's presentation of the Ten Commandments must be anti-moralistic in its conception and its method. The eminent Dominican theologian Romanus Cessario explains that there is nothing extraneous or imposed about the Ten Commandments: "Christian tradition has always affirmed that God has implanted in man the knowledge of the precepts contained in the Decalogue.

---

[21] Raniero Cantalamessa, *Life in Christ: A Spiritual Commentary on the Letter to the Romans* (Collegeville: The Liturgical Press, 2002), p. 2.

The natural law is promulgated in creation, and re-promulgated in privileged fashion in the precepts of the Decalogue: precepts that embody the actual intention of the lawgiver who is God himself." [22]

Pope John Paul II was eager to correct a common misconception about the Decalogue:

> The Ten Commandments are not an arbitrary imposition of a tyrannical Lord. They were written in stone; but before that, they were written on the human heart as the universal moral law, valid in every time and place. To keep the Commandments is to be faithful to ... ourselves, to our true nature and our deepest aspirations.... In revealing himself on the mountain and giving his law, God revealed man to man himself. [23]

Pope Benedict XVI, while a cardinal, as well has emphasized this nonmoralistic understanding of the Ten Commandments:

> Living out the Ten Commandments means living out our own resemblance to God, responding to the truth of our nature, and thus doing good. Living out the Ten Commandments means living out the divinity of man, and exactly that is freedom: the fusing of our being with the Divine Being and the resulting harmony of all with all.... If the Ten Commandments ... are the answer to the inner demands of our nature, then they are not at the opposite pole to our freedom but are rather the concrete form it takes. They are then the foundation for every law of freedom and are the one truly liberating power in human history. [24]

[22] Romanus Cessario et al., *The Love That Never Ends: A Key to the Catechism of the Catholic Church* (Huntington, Ind.: Our Sunday Visitor Press, 1996), pp. 109–10.

[23] Pope John Paul II, *Celebration of the Word at Mount Sinai* (Feb. 26, 2000).

[24] Joseph Cardinal Ratzinger, *Truth and Tolerance: Christian Belief and World Religions*, trans. Henry Taylor (San Francisco: Ignatius Press, 2004), pp. 253–55.

And during Pope Benedict's 2007 papal visit to Brazil, the Holy Father remarked that the Ten Commandments "lead to life, which means that they guarantee our authenticity. The commandments are not imposed upon us from without; they do not diminish our freedom. On the contrary: they are strong internal incentives leading us to act in a certain way." [25]

In terms of preparing people, then, what puts them in the right frame of mind to benefit best from preaching? The answer is an *attraction*. Giussani observes that "the motivation for saying 'yes' to something that comes into our life, defeating all preconceptions, is beauty." [26] Camus' keynote comment at the beginning of this chapter expresses it inversely: "You have to meet love before meeting morality. Otherwise it's torture." The point is that when a strong enough attraction takes hold of our lives, our Yes to what truly enriches our lives readily follows. Louis Lavelle explains that the good must be shown to us in order that we may be able to yield to the inclination that bears us toward it. Once we are struck by something appealing and desirable, we become docile, malleable, disponible . . . we change . . . we *want* to change. Because the proposal of the good *speaks to our elementary experience*. "The more a truth has to do with our life, the more easily it is seen with the naked eye." [27] We long to be like the good that we have experienced. As Saint Peter's preaching in chapter two of Acts proves, once hearers are swept up by a winning

[25] Pope Benedict XVI, "I Send You Out on the Great Mission of Evangelizing", Address to Youth, Pacaembu, Brazil (May 10, 2007).

[26] Luigi Giussani, quoted in Communion and Liberation, *The Miracle of a Change: Exercises of the Fraternity of Communion and Liberation* (Rimini, 1998), p. 16.

[27] Giussani, *Risk of Education*, p. 108.

attraction, they are eager to abandon their lives to "Gospel morality", that is, to the path that leads them to the fulfillment of their happiness.

That attraction is found principally in *the person* of the preacher. Father Vann writes, "When you have been shaken to the roots of your being by the mere presence of someone who stands for a truth, then you are impelled to examine the truth he stands for, and predisposed to apprehend it." [28] The first "message" of any preaching is the witness of the preacher—the winning attraction that he is because of his lived encounter with the living Christ. Without this personal witness, the chance for moral reform in the preacher's audience is not only impeded, it is thwarted. As Jean Vanier explains:

> The word can become a barrier. An alcoholic is told he must stop drinking; it's bad for his health. But he doesn't need to be told that—he's been vomiting all day. He doesn't need someone to proclaim the law to him, for he knows the law. What he wants is to find someone who will give him the force, the motivation, the thirst for life. It is not because you tell someone not to steal that he will not do it. He needs strength, he needs to be attached to someone who will give him the life and courage, the peace and love, which will help him not to steal, or not to take drugs, or not to drink, or not to fall into depression. [29]

This is why Dominican theologian Antonin Sertillanges says that "the function of an apostle is not, strictly speaking, to explain the truth—that is the professor's task—but to cause souls to confront the truth by doing so himself. The drama

---

[28] Vann, *Divine Pity*, p. 74.
[29] Jean Vanier, *Be Not Afraid* (Ramsey: Paulist Press, 1975), p. 95.

takes place in consciences."[30] And Father Cantalamessa adds: "The true Christian proclamation (the *kerygma*) does not consist in conveying propositions about the faith but in conveying the faith itself. Saying, 'Jesus is Lord' is saying something about oneself as well; it is the same as saying, 'Jesus is *my* Lord!' It goes without saying, therefore, that an intimate relationship with Jesus, made up of absolute devotion, deep friendship, and admiration, is the secret of the true proclaimer of the Gospel."[31]

An example of this dynamic from history: American authors Herman Melville and Nathaniel Hawthorne first came to meet each other while hiking in the Berkshire Mountains on August 5, 1850. A sudden thunderstorm sent them scurrying to the shelter of a rocky ledge where the two novelists began to discuss their respective literary work ... and to cement a great friendship. Hawthorne was the one who encouraged Melville to transform his real-life whaling adventures into a book. When *Moby-Dick* was published in 1851, Melville dedicated it to Hawthorne ... who read all seven hundred pages in two days and promptly sent the author a letter of exuberant praise. Upon reading it, Melville was moved to reply: "Knowing you persuades me more than the Bible of our immortality." *This* response is what the preacher's compelling witness makes possible in preaching.

Only once the congregation has been captivated by the winning attraction of the preacher can they be enjoined *to imitate* the good proposed in Sacred Scripture. The *Catechism* says clearly and emphatically: "*It is impossible* to keep

---

[30] Antonin Sertillanges, *Spirituality* (New York: McMullen Books, 1954), p. 178.
[31] Cantalamessa, *Mystery of God's Word*, p. 39.

the Lord's commandment by imitating the divine model *from outside*; there has to be *vital participation*, coming from the depths of the heart, in the holiness and mercy and the love of our God" (*CCC*, no. 2842; emphasis added). What is this "vital participation"? It is the "adoptive sonship" that is ours through the Holy Spirit. The imitation of Christ is possible only if a believer acknowledges himself to be an adopted child of God the Father—as one chosen and called to participate mysteriously in God's nature.

What is it that convinces people of their own mysterious participation in God's nature as adopted children? It is the certainty and conviction that spring up because of the *authority* of the preacher. The preacher's authority is perhaps the single most attractive aspect of any preacher. Monsignor Giussani says that true Christian authorities are people who "make you feel the memory of Christ ten times more easily than all the others". An authority is someone who makes it easier for us to perceive and experience Christ because of the extraordinary way that the authority acknowledges Jesus, obeys him, and makes the Event of Christ present as a "re-happening" of his Person. For such an authority is someone blessed with the ability to know our expectations and to answer our most urgent needs. An authority is a person who reopens our hearts, making us more present to our situation—to what is in front of us—intensifying our attention to reality, enabling us to recognize the Mystery. Through the experience of friendship with an authority, we reach a clear certainty by which "we free ourselves once and for all from the deception of moralism that many times makes us say, 'I can't do it, so it's not true.' We can look at this disarray, this fragility of ours, only in the company of another, accompanied by someone who has overcome it and who can help us to answer the question, to address this situation in which we all find ourselves." [32]

The encounter with authority helps us to discover our self and our deepest aspirations. Authority is supremely evocative for us since an authority is a person living life from the depths of his *I*, filled with a desire that arouses greater desire in us to live the same gusto and authenticity. The effect of authority is our vital participation in the holiness, mercy, and love of God. This vital participation in turn enables real imitation to happen. Saint Gregory of Nyssa makes the claim that "one receives the likeness of what he fixes his eyes on." The authority of the preacher is what makes him attractive in the first place; by beholding the authority of the preacher we receive his likeness. This is what Saint Paul summons us to do in I Corinthians 11:1 (and it is why it is *not* moralistic): "Be imitators of me, as I am of Christ."

The woman at the well was a person profoundly in need of conversion. Yet Christ does not begin his encounter with her by pronouncing commandments or by imposing moral "oughts"; rather, he offers the woman his friendship, his authority. Despite the immoral morass of her life, true morality was still at work in her because she lived continually directed toward something that was Other. The attraction of Christ provoked that in her. Thus, even when Christ exposes her evil, the woman does not feel condemned by it because she has discovered something even greater in her than her sin: Someone who desires true, pure union with her. Thanks to that Presence, her reformation is instantaneous, and she is suddenly a supremely moral person. The woman discovers at work in her a "real"

---

[32] Julián Carrón, quoted in Communion and Liberation, *Origin and Power of the "I": International Assembly of Communion and Liberation Responsibles*, La Thuile, Italy (Milan: Traces, 1999), p. 7.

morality: she loves, she wants to love; she is expecting and waiting for a Messiah who will love her out of her sad state. Moralism has turned the predicament of her life into squalid misery: she is outcast from society, she must gather water at the hottest, most brutal time of day, she is alone, she probably has been betrayed by her other loves. The rules haven't brought her any closer to the happiness she is now looking for in immorality. But all that changes when she encounters Jesus Christ.

The Implications for Preaching

1. In order for people to be persuaded to follow moral instruction that a preacher desires to give, the preacher must present himself as an *authority*. True morality is born as a liking for a person who is present to us—as the result of a *winning attraction*. The witness of the preacher's own friendship with Christ gives us the force, the motivation, and the thirst for a moral life. We can live Gospel morality when we have a bond with someone who gives us the courage to live life virtuously ... when we are united with an exemplar who fills our life with certainty and conviction. We need "vital participation" in order for virtuous imitation to be possible. As Saint Catherine of Siena reminds us, "First Christ acted, and from his actions he built the way. He taught you more by example than with words, always doing first what he talked about." This is what the people experienced when they listened to the preaching of John the Baptist. So transformed were they by the authority they experienced in the Baptist, the crowds, the tax collectors, and the soldiers begged John, "What shall we to do?" (Lk 3:10–14).

2.   In preaching to your people, do not ask the question "What are you to do?" without first addressing the question "Who are you?"

3.   In proposing a particular moral truth, the starting point must be its beauty. Once people are shown the good, they are then irresistibly drawn to follow it because they recognize how it corresponds to a crucial need of their hearts. Even the *Code of Canon Law* stresses this point where it says, "Christian doctrine is to be set forth *in a way accommodated to the condition of the listeners* and in a manner adapted to the needs of the times" (canon 769; emphasis added). However, it is never enough to propose merely the *message* of Christ, his teachings. Every moral instruction must lead to Christ's *Person*—to an encounter. Saint Gregory of Nyssa says, "Ideas create idols; only wonder leads to knowing." Preaching must be "wonder-ful".

4.   Be explicit about the agency of grace in the moral life. Preaching is less about *what* and more about *how*—How can we live for God alone? How is it possible for me, with all my limitations and defects, to live in a saintly way? Gospel preaching emphasizes that it is Christ who desires this for us, and it is Christ who carries it out—overcoming the that's-just-the-way-I-am heresy: "Christ enables us *to live in him* all that he himself lived, and *he lives it in us*" (*CCC*, no. 521).

5.   Be very attentive to the "bottom line" in your preaching: if the final concrete proposal of your preaching puts the initiative on the hearer rather than on God and grace, it is moralistic. You cannot exhort us to imitate

anyone if we are not first convinced that we are God's children. The implicit and explicit inducement of all Gospel preaching is this: "Look at what God is doing in your life . . . what is happening. Look at who you are!"

6. In terms of the tone and delivery of preaching that conveys moral instruction, keep in mind the observation of Father Maurice Zundel: "Man is enlightened by tenderness." As Saint Claude de la Colombière declared, "I find no sinner in the entire Gospel story who was induced to repent by anything other than gentleness and kindness." Be wary of words like "should", "strive", and their ilk. In terms of your presentation, don't speak *at* the people but *to* them, personally and compassionately like a loving father.

7. The ultimate, consummate exhortation of any preaching directly addressing moral issues is that of Christ himself: Remain in Jesus. The supreme end of preaching is to liberate people from whatever keeps them closed off to God, shackled in shame, blackmailed by sin and their own imperfection. The only way that happens is by the risen Jesus coming face to face with us and asking, "Do you love me?" We preach to generate in others the ability to say, "Yes, Lord, you know that I love you . . . despite all my betrayal, failure, cowardice, and hypocrisy—you know that I do love you. And because of this preaching, now *I* know it too."

Conclusion

One of my favorite *New Yorker* cartoons pictures a pastor standing outside his church greeting his parishioners after

the Sunday service. His sermon apparently overstressed the
prospect of eternal damnation; the exiting faithful all have
disgruntled looks on their faces. One man shakes the minister's hand. As he does so, he says, "To hell with you, too."
Moralism fails again.

Father Cantalamessa provides an apt summary of our
discussion of moralism, authentic morality, and Gospel
preaching:

> We must put forth in the Catholic Church ... a procla-
> mation that, like that of Jesus, does not begin with duties
> and commandments but with the gift of God, with grace,
> not from what man must do but from what God has done
> for him. Peter did not begin to speak, saying immediately,
> "Repent and be baptized!" No, first he proclaimed Christ
> crucified and risen and made Lord; then, when hearts were
> open and ready to receive it, he launched the appeal to
> penitence and change of life.[33]

[33] Raniero Cantalamessa, *The Mystery of Pentecost* (Collegeville, Minn.: Liturgical Press, 2001), pp. 28–29.

CHAPTER 6

The Fruit of the Encounter:

Preaching Is Regenerating

"I became your father in Christ Jesus through the gospel."

—SAINT PAUL (1 Cor 4:15)

I STILL REMEMBER word for word one of the most brilliant homilies that I ever heard ... even though it was preached over twenty-seven years ago. The homilist was Dominican Father Clem Burns, and the Gospel was the episode of the woman caught in adultery. Here's the homily: "All the other people went away. The woman stayed with Jesus."

Why do I remember that homily? Yes, it was short, and, yes, it was profound and eloquent. But I have heard a lot of brief, moving homilies in my life ... and I cannot remember one of them at the moment. Yet this one I cannot help but remember. Why? Because Father Clem's preaching regenerated me. I was transformed by this homily. Every time I recall it—and all it implies—I become more human. It was not simply his inspired interpretation of the Scriptural text; it was equally the authenticity and authority of his personal, priestly witness of faith that moved and humanized me. I knew that *he* stayed with Jesus; that is why his homily proposing that we do the same was so compelling. This is what made that encounter of his preaching unforgettable for me.

The Primordial Search for the Father

Our essential interest in preaching—what we are looking for from it—is correlative to an impulse central to the human condition, namely, the search for *the father*. The late Joseph Campbell, one of the world's chief scholars of mythology, in his book *The Power of Myth*, maintained that the pursuit of the father has to do with finding one's own character and destiny. He held that it is the discovery of one's destiny that is symbolized by the father quest.

This drive to know and to be united with our father—a theme predominant in literature since Homer—has remained a preoccupation for people down through the ages ... even for those who had bad or absent fathers. A powerful book entitled *Lost in the Victory: Reflections of American War Orphans of World War II* presents the collected reflections of more than two dozen self-described orphans of World War II, who relate what it means to have lost their fathers. Decades after the end of the war, these orphans (when the book was published, they were adults in their fifties) still urgently feel the need to connect with their fathers. One World War II orphan, a woman named Kathleen Eaton, expresses it poignantly: "Sometimes before I fall asleep, or on his birthday, Father's Day, or a holiday, I ache for him. I want to hear his voice, smell his aftershave, watch him eat, write a letter, shave, comb his hair, and to hold me. Growing up, I could feel him close to me, like a guardian angel. I would talk to him in my head.... I think about him every day, and still I feel he guards me." [1]

No matter whether our father is living or dead, the quest to be united with the father never dies. And if it cannot be satisfied by our own biological father, then we persist in our pursuit until we find a substitute father to take his place. The search for the father expresses the need in us to be regenerated.

Eaton's words give an incisive first hint of what I mean by "being regenerated". We need someone in our life to whom we belong, to whom we can feel close in a personal, specific, and unique way; the presence of the one who regenerates us is a protective one that accompanies us, guards us, assures us, makes us feel secure; the presence of the one who regenerates us is so close that we can "talk to him in our head"—we might say that the one who regenerates us moves us to pray.

It seems that nothing can undo this urge in us. The author Albert Camus, one of modernity's foremost proponents of the theory of absurdism, was killed in an automobile accident at the age of forty-seven. When those who found him sorted through the wreckage of his car, they discovered one hundred forty-four manuscript pages that Camus had written—all of them about his search for his father (who was mortally wounded as a soldier in World War I when Camus was but a year old). Apparently Camus' search for his father was a stronger force in him than the conscious awareness of the senselessness of everything around him (i.e., absurdism). What was Camus looking for? Was he hoping by his search in some way to be regenerated?

---

[1] Susan J. Hadler and Ann Bennett Mix, *Lost in the Victory: Reflections of American War Orphans of World War II*, ed. Calvin L. Christman (Denton, Tex.: University of North Texas Press, 1998), p. 213.

We are. Why do we go to church and subject ourselves to preaching? Why do we bother—even dare—to approach an occupied pulpit? What are we looking for? One thing is for certain: we are not merely in pursuit of a conveyed knowledge, an exchange of ideas. Pope Benedict XVI has told us emphatically: "Being Christian is not the result of a lofty idea." And, anyway, if I need information, I don't go to a pulpit; I go to Google. There are far more convenient, expedient, and comprehensive ways of gaining the data I need about God and faith than preaching. I don't listen to preaching to lay hold of facts; I give myself to preaching to be embraced by a Presence.

People put themselves at the disposal of a preacher expecting to be *moved*. By this I do not mean anything sentimental or emotional. The "movement" we seek for ourselves in preaching is something far more existential— something ontological. I go to hear preaching impelled by the awareness that what I need to be fully myself I do not have inside me and I cannot bring it about. What I require must be given to me from outside. I put myself before a preacher filled with the expectation that *it will* be given to me . . . that God's Word contains—and will furnish—what I need to be myself. I go to preaching compelled by the hope that my life can be better, that I can become more fully alive, that I can be more complete. I approach preaching in search of a new purpose, a new possibility, a new power, taking a risk on a new positivity and optimism. I go to preaching awaiting a new energy, a new capacity, a new fervor. I go looking forward to being changed, revived, reformed, repaired, recharged, restored. I go to preaching to be regenerated.

I dispose myself to preaching because I need to be rescued from the nihilism of the world that oppresses me to the point of suffocation. This is why Pope Benedict XVI, in a forthright and almost blunt way, insists in *Sacramentum Caritatis*: "Generic and abstract homilies should be avoided. In particular, I ask these ministers to preach in such a way that the homily closely relates the proclamation of the Word of God to the sacramental celebration and the life of the community, *so that the Word of God truly becomes the Church's vital nourishment and support*" (no. 46; emphasis added). I go to preaching so that something vital will be carried out in me that I cannot bring about myself by which I become the person I am destined to be. I subject myself to the event of preaching so that I can be perfect even as the heavenly Father is perfect. But in order to possess that Fatherly perfection, I must be regenerated by a father.

The Preacher Is a Father

Preaching is parental. Pope John Paul II in *Pastores Dabo Vobis* (I Will Give You Shepherds) describes priestly ministry in a maternal way: the priest must be "capable of bearing 'the pangs of birth' until 'Christ be formed' in the faithful" (no. 22). Saint Thomas Aquinas makes the point that "through teaching and preaching a man acquires the dignity of a father, whence they who instruct spiritually are called fathers" (*In Matt.*, chap. 1). We are expecting to meet this father when we place ourselves before a pulpit, for nothing less than a father's paternal solicitude and strength can resolve our predicament.

When the prodigal son of the famous Lucan parable finally hits bottom, he ends up talking to himself and says: "I will arise and return to my father." On the verge of despair, the prodigal son realizes that the most reasonable thing for him to do is return to his father. But why, of all people, his *father* as a last resort? Because the prodigal son knows that, in his hopeless situation, what he needs is nothing less than the person who can restore his life and regenerate him. And that person is the one who generated him in the first place: his father. We are allowed to eavesdrop on the prodigal's soliloquy so that we will get the clue that returning to the father is what we need to do too. We do so when we participate in the event of preaching.

In his book *A Father Who Keeps His Promises*, Scott Hahn tells a true story that poignantly illustrates the indispensable human dependence on fathers. In 1989, an earthquake registering 8.2 on the Richter scale ravaged the country of Armenia, killing thirty thousand people. Among the countless buildings reduced to rubble was a grammar school filled with students. A young father raced to the place where the school once stood and gazed aghast at the horrific pile of debris. But only for a moment, because then he started digging in the wreckage with his bare hands. Someone tried to stop him, saying, "They're all dead." The father replied, "You can grumble, or you can help me lift these bricks." And the determined father continued to dig for twelve, twenty-four, thirty-six hours. Thirty-eight hours later, from the darkness the father heard a muffled groan. It was his own son Armand. The father pulled the boy from the ruins along with thirteen other children—at which Armand turned to his classmates and said: "See, I told you my father wouldn't forget us." [2]

It is the prospect of a father who comes to save us from the darkness that has collapsed around us that keeps us alive,

[2] Scott Hahn, *A Father Who Keeps His Promises* (Cincinnati: Servant Publications, 1998), p. 14.

that keeps us hoping, that keeps us holding out for a second chance. This is the role of the preacher. The preacher of the Gospel ministers in the Church to give us the assurance that, no matter what the calamity we may face, we have not been forgotten. The preacher is there to pull us from the ruins of our lives. Saint John of the Cross puts it plainly: "The preacher's voice must possess the power to raise a dead man from his sepulcher." [3]

Preaching is one of the preeminent ways that the priest-preacher exercises his vocation as father. The night before he dies, Jesus names one of our most terrifying fears and vows to protect us from it; he promises, "I will not leave you orphans" (Jn 14:18, NAB). Christ keeps his promise by endowing the Church with priests, fathers ordained to preach, whose preaching regenerates us so that we become the People of God.

Notice how the legendary Dominican preacher Saint Vincent Ferrer (d. 1419) insists on metaphors about generating as integral to his instruction on effective preaching:

> In preaching use simple, familiar language to explain in detail what ought to be done. Support your contentions as much as possible with examples that will strike the sinner entangled in the sins of which you speak, *as if you were preaching to him alone.* Comport yourself, however, in such wise that your words may not seem to proceed from a proud spirit or one impelled by anger, but rather from the bowels of charity and *a paternal love. Let people find in you a father full of compassion for his children* when they sin or are grievously ill or *fall into the deep pit whence he seeks to extricate them. Have rather the heart of a mother who caresses her children,* rejoicing in their progress and in the glory of paradise which she hopes for them. It is by such

[3] St. John of the Cross, *The Ascent of Mount Carmel*, book III, chap. 45.

preaching that one becomes useful to one's hearers; whereas, by merely speaking to them of the vices and virtues in general one scarcely touches them all.[4]

We go to preaching, like the desolate prodigal son on his way home, in the hopes of finding a receptive father who will welcome us, have mercy on us, and give us what we need to live again. The way that Monsignor Massimo Camisasca describes fatherhood applies in a particularly apt way to the regenerative role of the priest-preacher:

> This is the task of a father, a master, a teacher: to stay beside his son, his friend, his disciple, in order to open his eyes that he might give names to things, and to teach his hands to write and create and his feet to walk forward. A father or a master desires to help the son or disciple truly to "meet" himself and what is around him. He wants to make him walk on the earth without forgetting the stars, to help him to understand that desires are not the sign of unreachable dreams which a bad god put into our hearts. They are rather the imprint of him who desired us into being from nothing and who never leaves us on our own.[5]

However, such fatherly care can seem very far from us, weighed down as we are by our fallenness. For, as Pope John Paul II recognized, "original sin attempts to abolish fatherhood, destroying its rays which permeate the created world, placing in doubt the truth about God who is Love and leaving man only with a sense of the master-slave relationship."[6] In response, the Church gives us back the very thing that original sin conspires to take away:

---

[4] St. Vincent Ferrer, O.P., *A Treatise on the Spiritual Life*, chap. 12; emphasis added.

[5] Massimo Carnisasca, *Fraternity and Mission* (newsletter; Rome, June, 2003), p. 1.

[6] Pope John Paul II, *Crossing the Threshold of Hope* (New York: Knopf, 1995), p. 228.

fatherhood. We are liberated from the tyranny of slavery and doubt by the gift of someone who loves us as a father: the priest-preacher whose love in the form of preaching regenerates our original relationship with God and alleviates the effects of original sin.

"The *cura pastoralis* or *cura animarum* ... is proper to the office of parish priest and principally expressed by preaching the Word of God.... The great value of the spiritual paternity of the parish priest in his parish is clearly evident." [7] In the light of this fact, the *Code of Canon Law* insists that "sacred ministers, among whose principal duties is the proclamation of the Gospel of God to all, are to hold the function of preaching in esteem since the people of God are first brought together by the Word of the living God" (canon 762). What original sin connives to abolish, the Church deliberately reconstitutes by ordaining men as priest-fathers whose regenerative preaching delivers us from the despotism of original sin. Through the regenerating preaching of a priest-father, the rays of God's Fatherhood once again permeate the world.

What It Means to Be Regenerated

To be regenerated is to encounter a love that re-creates us. To be regenerated is to know that we are loved by an Other whose love addresses and fulfills our deepest longings—not because of *our* goodness but because of *his*. The love that regenerates invests us with unprecedented ability. When I am loved in a totalizing way, I feel that I can do anything.

[7] Congregation for the Clergy, *The Priest, Pastor and Leader of the Parish Community* (2002), no. 19.

To be regenerated is to belong. When we are regenerated we know we are not alone. To be regenerated is to be rescued from our isolation, our alienation, our loneliness. It is to recognize the companionship that precedes our solitude. I can live at the level of my *I* because I have been blessed with the assurance of the Presence of a You. I am in a relationship with the Infinite who loves me. To be regenerated means to recognize that communion is our destiny. I am part of a belonging that defines me.

To be regenerated is to be blessed with the conviction that life has a meaning. We see reason in reality and purpose in life. When we are regenerated, our freedom is revitalized, re-launched. We are given identity, mission, joy, freshness, gladness. We are able to read the abundant signs in reality that point to the Infinite. We recognize that fulfillment is possible; hope remains the most reasonable position to hold in facing the world. That all-encompassing attitude of hope counteracts the anxiety, doubt, chaos, despondency, and dread that scheme to prevail. When we are regenerated, nihilism cannot win.

To be regenerated is to realize that our self-esteem is not based on our efforts—on what we have done or accomplished. Rather, I live moved by the understanding that my self-worth is based squarely on the fact that *I am loved*. To be regenerated is to refuse to be scandalized by the reality of our own fragility.

When we are regenerated, we are lifted up out of our concupiscence, liberated from our fears, from our insecurities and inadequacy, our cynicism and impenetrability. Being regenerated keeps us from closing in on ourselves, from giving way to idolatrous self-reliance, from capitulating to the urgings of original sin. One of the defining properties of any true father is that a father refuses to become fatalistic about his child's failures. When we are regenerated by a father-figure, we see ourselves the way that he sees us. For the one who regenerates us, regenerates *in* us an ability to face the perils and terrors of life. At a talk, professor of psychology Paul Vitz told a true story about some elementary-school-age brothers and sisters who had become frightened during a thunderstorm. Their father had not been present. Later when their father returned home, the little children rushed to give their report to him about the terrifying storm, saying: "If you had been here, we would not have been afraid." When we are regenerated, even otherwise frightful things are not scary.

To be regenerated is to be endowed with an infallible certainty. This certainty conquers the forgetfulness, the weakness, and the inconstancy in us. It goes beyond any limitations arising from original sin. For this certainty is not something that we manufacture; rather, certainty is something that enters our lives and bonds us to it. Certainty is Someone who has happened to us. This certainty has at its root the entrusting of ourselves to Christ offered to me by the one who regenerates—it flows from the fact that *we are chosen*. Certainty springs up from the Presence of God, and not from my ability. The more I am regenerated, the more my certainty flourishes. For when I am regenerated, then even when I am confronted by my weakness, I refuse to obsess about my (undeniable) deficiency— instead, I keep looking at Jesus. Certainty comes from that gaze. Monsignor Giussani says that the meaning of the Church "lies in the fact that it enables man to attain a certainty about Christ".[8] This is why Saint Thomas Aquinas

[8] Luigi Giussani, *Why the Church?* (Montreal: McGill-Queen's University Press, 2001), p. 8.

says that to anyone having faith, the omnipotence and mercy of God are certainties.

When we are regenerated, we want to depend on the one who regenerates us. When we are regenerated, we lose interest in self-absorption, in self-assertion, in self-sufficiency. We let down our guard of individualistic independence. We want to stay close to the one who regenerates us, to deepen our relationship with that person, to become more sensitive and aware of what that person has to offer. We desire to make our life one of attentive listening and holy obedience—of union. It is children who know that they are loved and accepted just the way they are who are most eager to change and to conform more and more to a father and mother who love them. When we are regenerated, our affection is expressed in such an appropriate, holy dependence—in a gift of self—for we recognize that to be ourselves we need another.

The *Catechism* sums up succinctly what it means to be regenerated: when we are regenerated, we are imbued with *"parrhesia*, straightforward simplicity, filial trust, joyous assurance, humble boldness, the certainty of being loved" (*CCC*, no. 2778). And this process of regeneration must remain ongoing, progressive, always advancing. Raïssa Maritain, wife of the philosopher Jacques Maritain, wrote in her journal: "Looking at the photograph of a sculpture in Chartres Cathedral, God molding Adam, I'm drawn to recollection by the thought that our very loving Father continues to mold us like that right up to the day when our perfection is achieved in heaven."[9] Preaching has been instituted in the Church to bring all this about.

[9] Raïssa Maritain, *Raïssa's Journal* (Albany: Magi, 1974), p. 43.

Jesus instructs us: we are to change and become like little children in order to enter the Kingdom of God, for whoever becomes like a little child is of greatest importance (Mt 18:3–4). In other words, Christ commands that we be regenerated. And Christ *can* command such a change because his Presence makes that regeneration happen. The possibility of that transformation for people today remains a reality precisely because of the pastoral ministry of priest-preachers eager to exercise their spiritual fatherhood. Thanks to regenerative preaching, we receive a spirit of adoption through which we cry out, "Abba! Father!" (Rom 8:15–16). Through preaching that regenerates, the promise of the One seated on the throne comes true: "I will be his God and he shall be my son" (Rev 21:7).

This regenerative dimension of preaching is evident in the way that Saint Albert the Great identifies the end of preaching. He says that "the fruit consequent on preaching is fivefold. The first is the confession of sin. The second, following from this, is interior beauty and truth. The third, holiness of life; the fourth, greatness of works. The fifth is the desire and affection for eternal things and the contemplation of them" (*In Psal.* XCV, 9). Saint Thomas Aquinas makes a similar assessment, stating that the purpose of preaching is "first to illuminate the intellect, secondly, to sweeten the passions, thirdly, for the raising up of love, fourthly, for the rectitude of works, fifthly, for the attainment of glory, sixthly, for the instruction of others" (*In Isaias*, chap. 49).

The assurance that we priests can preach in a manner that regenerates others is the fact of our being configured to Jesus Christ. In speaking about the preaching ministry of Christ, then–Cardinal Ratzinger made the point that "Jesus' proclamation was never mere preaching, mere words;

it was 'sacramental,' in the sense that his words were and are inseparable from his 'I'—from his 'flesh'." [10] We can regenerate others when we preach precisely because we partake of that *I* of Christ right to our flesh—"This is my body." As Saint John Eudes puts it: "All that is [Christ's] is yours: his spirit, his heart, his body and soul, and all his faculties. You must make use of all these as of your own, to serve, praise, love, and glorify God" (quoted in the *Catechism*, no. 1698).

Preaching is regenerating: "The Gospel preached by the Church is not just a message but *a divine and life-giving experience* for those who believe, hear, receive, and obey the message." [11]

As John Henry Cardinal Newman says, "one thing is necessary—an intense perception and appreciation of the end for which he preaches, and that is to be the minister of some definite spiritual good to those who hear him. Who could wish to be more eloquent, more powerful, more successful than the Teacher of the Nations? Yet who more earnest, who more natural, who more unstudied, who more self-forgetting than he?" [12]

Examples from the New Testament

When Jesus preaches and ministers, people are regenerated. Sometimes the verification of it appears concretely in the explicit way that Christ addresses the people he regenerates.

---

[10] Joseph Cardinal Ratzinger, *Gospel, Catechesis, Catechism: Sidelights on the "Catechism of the Catholic Church"* (San Francisco: Ignatius Press, 1997), p. 50.

[11] Congregation for the Clergy, *The Priest and the Third Christian Millennium, Teacher of the Word, Minister of the Sacraments, and Leader of the Community* (1999), no. 2.1; emphasis added.

[12] John Henry Newman, *The Idea of a University* (Notre Dame: Notre Dame University Press, 1982), part 2, art. 6.2, p. 306.

For example, when four friends lower a paralyzed man through a roof in the hope of gaining a healing for him from Jesus, the Lord calls the paralytic "my son" (Mt 9:2 and parallels). After healing the woman with the hemorrhage, Jesus calls the woman—who perhaps was his age or older—"daughter" (Mk 5:34 and parallels). When the rich young man rejects Christ's offer to be regenerated, Jesus turns to those remaining with him—those who have been regenerated by him—and says, "Children, how hard it is ... to enter the kingdom of God" (Mk 10:24). For to enter the Kingdom of God, one must accept it as a child (Lk 18:17)—that is, one must be willing to be regenerated.

The Lord emphasizes this principal truth of the Gospel again and again when he teaches that to welcome a child is to welcome Christ himself (Mk 9:36–37); when he states that the Kingdom of God belongs to children (Mk 10:14); when he warns that getting into the Kingdom requires that we change radically and become like children, i.e., be regenerated (Mt 18:1–5); when he informs us that the great truths held by the heavenly Father will be revealed to the merest children, that is, to those who allow themselves to be regenerated (Lk 10:21). With this in mind, we see with new eyes the deepest significance of the fact that the Evangelist John states in the first verses of his Gospel: "To all who received him ... he gave power to become children of God" (Jn 1:12); to accept Christ is to be regenerated. And in the last chapter of John, as if to substantiate this opening claim of John's Gospel, we hear the risen Christ call his disciples "children" (Jn 21:5).

Of course, what stupefies us most about the 180-degree change we witness in the Samaritan woman at the well is precisely the regeneration that takes place in her through her encounter with Christ. This consummately cynical and nihilistic woman must have had a special suspicion of and loathing for men. But somehow the love that she experiences in Jesus Christ manages to pierce the callus of her life. Even the exposure of her considerable sins cannot dull the liberation and new life she experiences in meeting Jesus. The proof of the titanic change in the woman is her certainty. She goes off, leaving her old life behind, proclaiming to the people of the town, "Come, see a man who told me all that I ever did!" That is, the woman regenerates others. Formerly, the people scorned this woman who was a blight to their community. But now they are won over by her conviction, her humble boldness, her joyous assurance, her mission. "So when the Samaritans came to him, they asked him to stay with them; and he stayed there two days" (Jn 5:40). To be regenerated is to desire to stay close to the one who regenerates us.

Another example: Why was King Herod so reluctant to have John the Baptist executed? One would think that, with the turmoil John was causing in the king's "domestic" life, Herod would have been happy to dispense with the Baptist. But "Herod feared John, knowing that he was a righteous and holy man, and kept him safe. When he heard him, he was much perplexed; and yet he heard him gladly" (Mk 6:20). That is, Herod was beginning to be regenerated by John. Film director Franco Zeffirelli captured this dimension of the relationship between John the Baptist and King Herod brilliantly in his film *Jesus of Nazareth*. In handing over John to execution, Herod reacted as if he were losing his father.

The *Catechism* repeatedly refers to baptism as "the sacrament of regeneration" (see nos. 556, 784, 1141, 1213, 1215, 1262, 2345). Over and over again in the New Testament, the preaching of the apostles results in the regeneration of baptism. "Those who received [Peter's] word were baptized, and there were added that day about three thousand souls" (Acts 2:41). In Samaria, Philip encountered Simon the magician—a shyster who passed himself off as a V.I.P. while managing to hold spellbound people from every rank of society. Philip responded by preaching the Gospel. "They listened to [Simon], because for a long time he had amazed them with his magic. But when they believed Philip as he preached good news about the kingdom of God and the name of Jesus Christ, they were baptized, both men and women. Even Simon himself believed, and after being baptized he continued with Philip. And seeing signs and great miracles performed, he was amazed" (Acts 8:11–13). Philip worked the same regenerating effect on the pilgrim Ethiopian who, upon hearing Philip interpret Sacred Scripture for him, pleaded, "What is to prevent my being baptized?" (Acts 8:26–40).

A Most Famous Example

The young Augustine of Hippo was a man of towering intellect who had developed a repugnance for Christianity. His disdain was in reaction to an odious biblical fundamentalism he had come across in certain presenters of the faith. Despite his unparalleled brilliance, something more than rigorous logic (or moralism!) was required to bring this self-absorbed skeptic into the life of the Church. As Augustine himself recalls, what he needed was a regenerating presence. He found it in Saint Ambrose, Bishop of Milan.

> This man of God, Ambrose, received me like a father and, as bishop, told me how glad he was that I had come. My heart warmed to him, not at first as a teacher of the truth,

which I had quite despaired of finding in your Church, but simply as a man who showed me kindness.... Although I did not trouble to take what Ambrose said to heart, but only to listen to the manner in which he said it—this being the only paltry interest that remained to me now that I had lost hope that man could find the path that led to you—nevertheless his meaning, which I tried to ignore, found its way into my mind together with his words, which I admired so much. I could not keep the two apart, and while I was all ears to seize upon his eloquence, I also began to sense the truth of what he said, though only gradually.... These passages had been death to me when I took them literally, but once I heard them explained in their spiritual meaning I began to blame myself for my despair.[13]

Look at what a close reading of this pregnant passage from Augustine's *Confessions* reveals. What struck Augustine first of all was that Ambrose received him like a *father*. Even though Ambrose, like Augustine, was a man with a monumental mind, it was not Ambrose as teacher that impressed the jaded young Augustine. Rather, what impressed him was the fact that such a distinguished and outstanding person would extend himself to Augustine in a most paternal, approachable manner—"simply as a man"—showing him kindness (Zundel: man is enlightened by tenderness).

Augustine's heart warmed simply because Ambrose was "glad ... that [he] had come". Augustine began to be regenerated when he recognized how much Ambrose valued his mere presence. Ambrose offered a welcome devoid of any judgment or moralism. In the simple experience of being together with Ambrose, Augustine began to become his true self.

---

[13] Augustine of Hippo, *Confessions*, trans. R. S. Pine-Coffin (New York: Penguin, 1961), pp. 107–8.

By his own admission, Augustine went to Ambrose with a radically closed mind: he had "despaired of finding truth in your Church". But because of Ambrose's winning attraction, Augustine could no longer ignore the meaning of Ambrose's proposal, which found its way into Augustine's mind. In being regenerated, Augustine threw off his nihilism; the irresistibility of the truth had won him over. Regenerated by both the content and the method of Ambrose's preaching, Augustine began to seize the truth of what Ambrose said.

With that, Augustine's heart—his *I*—began to come alive. By his own admission, he had been living with a reduced heart. The only desire left in him was his "paltry interest" in rhetoric, for Augustine was himself a professional rhetoretician. But God used this desire to draw Augustine to Ambrose and thereby to awaken his heart and reignite his desire. Beauty regenerated him.

And—much as we saw with the story of Helen Keller—the moment of being regenerated brings with it an experience of remorse for Augustine. In the face of the meaning that he had come to experience, thanks to his encounter with Ambrose, Augustine confesses: "I began to blame myself for my despair." He is blessed with a new and true way of judging reality.

From our knowledge of the rest of the story, we know that Augustine remained close to Ambrose, depended upon him, was obedient to him, and let himself be formed by him. Augustine purposefully included this account of his regenerating encounter with Ambrose in his *Confessions* as a way of living *memory*—so that the event of his being regenerated could re-happen for him and also for us. To this day the Church continues to reap the rich fruits of Augustine's regeneration by Ambrose. There are more citations by Saint Augustine in the *Catechism of the Catholic Church* than by anyone else.

The Implications for Preaching

1. Be mindful of what people desire from preaching. They come to church like the prodigal son returning home profoundly needy, hoping for a second chance at life; they want to be regenerated. They are in search of their own character and destiny.

2. Whether they realize it or not, people are expecting a preacher to be a father, that is, someone who will regenerate them. The *Catechism* reminds us: "You have not given yourself faith as you have not given yourself life.... I cannot believe without being carried by the faith of others, and by my faith I help support others in the faith" (*CCC*, no. 166). People will put their trust in a preacher if they are confident that he can be counted on to rescue them from the rubble of their lives (Scott Hahn); to extricate them from the deep pit into which they have fallen (Saint Vincent Ferrer); to raise the dead from their tombs (Saint John of the Cross). The efficacy of your spiritual paternity as priest extends especially to your preaching: "Preaching is a grace that causes grace.... Through the instrumentality of a discourse proceeding from grace, the hearer is offered the grace to receive the 'word of grace' (Acts 20:32) and to conform himself to its demands." [14] The preacher, being himself conformed

---

[14] Dominic Rover, O.P., "Preaching, III (Theology of)", *New Catholic Encyclopedia*, vol. 11 (Washington, D.C.: Catholic University of America Press, 1967), pp. 697–701.

to Christ, "begets" other souls in Christ. The reason why people so often seek out a particular priest for confession is because that priest, as a spiritual father, regenerated them through his preaching. He is a man to be trusted with the most delicate of matters.

3. Keep in mind that Sacred Scripture intends to regenerate. "You have been born anew, not of perishable seed but from imperishable, through the living and abiding word of God" (1 Pet 1:23). In your *lectio divina* in preparation for preaching, search the text from the perspective of how it intends to regenerate. What is the Scripture addressing in human experience? How does it capture the "problem" of being human? How does it initiate and effect an encounter? How does it concretely offer new life to those who receive it?

4. In order to protect preaching from becoming generic or abstract, everything that the preacher proposes has to be verified in his own experience. If what he says is true, then necessarily it is true in his own life and it can be verified concretely. To ensure this, Saint Augustine offers this counsel: "When the hour is come that he must speak, the preacher ought, before he opens his mouth, to lift up his thirsty soul to God, to drink in what he is about to pour forth, and to be himself filled with what he is about to distribute" (*De Doctrina Christiana*, bk. 4, chap. 15). For no one can regenerate unless he is being regenerated. The priest needs the companionship of good friends to support his humanity and therefore his ministry. As Saint Thérèse of Lisieux realized, "If love ceased to function, the apostles would forget to preach the Gospel" (St. Thérèse of Lisieux,

Autobiography of a Saint, trans. Ronald Knox [London: Harvill, 1958], p. 235, quoted in the *Catechism*, no. 826).

5. Regenerate others through the very manner of your preaching. Of course, the most effective way to do this is not to use a text when you preach. It is hard if not impossible to connect with people if the preacher is tied to a physical text. You do not use a text when you hear confessions, and yet you do very well in speaking a regenerating word on the spot to people in real need. Also, take advantage of the new allowance granted in the 2000 revision of the *Institutio Generalis Missalis Romani* permitting the priest to give the homily "standing at the chair or at the ambo, or, when appropriate, *in another suitable place*" (no. 136). This privilege gives the preacher access to the most prime position in the sanctuary for interaction with the people and, thus, for regenerating them.

6. Have the effects of regenerating clearly in mind as you prepare your homily, especially certainty, new purpose, gladness, and hope. Very often you can see these effects on the faces of your people immediately after Mass—regeneration happens that quickly. The more you are mindful of the concrete change you intend to generate in your people, the better chance your preaching stands of being an effective instrument for bringing it about.

Conclusion

The paradigm for preaching as regenerating is found in the grateful father of the returned prodigal son. As he proclaims the event of his son's regeneration, we in turn are regenerated by those saving words: "He was dead, but has come back to life." Our persistent need to be regenerated is summed up trenchantly by Pope John Paul II in one of his plays in which a character declares: "One must enter the radiation of fatherhood, since only there does everything become fully real." [15] Thanks to the preaching of the Church, we can do just that.

[15] Karol Wojtyła, *The Radiation of Fatherhood*, Part I, Scene 5, in *The Collected Plays and Writings on Theater*, trans. Boleslaw Taborski (Berkeley: University of California Press, 1987), p. 341.

CHAPTER 7

The Habit of Preaching:

Some Pragmatics

*"There is something more than composition in a sermon; there is
something personal in preaching; people are drawn and moved, not
simply by what is said, but by how it is said, and who says it."*

—VEN. JOHN HENRY NEWMAN

WHAT CAN I DO to preach better? When a priest friend
recently asked me this question, I could not help but
think he was already on his way to becoming a great
preacher ... because God can work wonders with that
desire. This, as you know, is not a how-to book on preaching, but perhaps a few words on the pragmatics of preaching would concretize what we have said about preaching
as regenerating in order to help put it into practice.

Begin at the beginning ... of the week. Start your *lectio
divina* for next Sunday's homily as early as you can, that is,
as soon as you have finished preaching this Sunday's homily. But certainly begin no later than Monday. Great homilies get that way because they have had time to simmer,
to mature. The earlier you begin your homily preparation,

the stronger will be the certainty you will radiate when you preach.

Even if you use the lectionary, a missal, or *Magnificat* to prepare, be sure to work with a Bible as well in order to get a sense of the greater context of the passage under consideration, to discover if any verses have been omitted, to compare the passage with its parallels, etc.

Read the text out loud. It is amazing the number of things you will discover in a text when you read it aloud as opposed to just scanning the words on a printed page (with which you may be overly familiar). Praying the text out loud provides the added benefit of auricular reinforcement. James Fallows, writing for *The Atlantic Monthly*, comments:

> You can take things in much faster with the eye, but they seem more likely to stay if they come by ear. Perhaps this is because aural signals seem to connect more-varied stimuli to more regions of the brain than the sight of print does. After all, a three-second passage from any familiar piece of music—The Beach Boys' "I Get Around," "It's a Small World," "Gaudeamus Igitur"—instantly calls up not only the rest of the music but also, often, the sights, smells, and emotions of associated events. It's hard to think of a written paragraph with the same broad power.... Anything that comes through the ear has a chance of sticking, but some combinations of voice and word are so effective that, like music, they are practically impossible to forget.[1]

Work from a sole sheet of paper. Make a deal with yourself that all of your homily preparation notes will have to fit on just a single sheet of paper (one side). It is a challenge, but the discipline will be a great advantage because

---

[1] James Fallows, "Reading by Ear" in *The Atlantic Monthly*, 287, no. 1 (January 2001): 16–17.

it will force you to make a judgment about what is absolutely critical for you to include in your preparation and therefore in your preaching itself. This one piece of paper sets the parameters within which you must work.

Copy out lines of the Scriptural text. On your single sheet of paper, write out phrases that strike you from the Scripture under consideration beginning with the Gospel. These do not have to be complete sentences but rather units that are meaningful to you (what playwrights call "beats"). When we transcribe the Scripture for ourselves, we begin to see connections, parallels, contrasts, repeated words and phrases, inconsistencies, symbols, nuances, and other distinctive and conspicuous elements that might otherwise go unnoticed.

The writing process engages a deep part of one's self and unleashes the creative process. As Father Michael Casey points out, "The act of writing is itself a meditation—a way of assimilating what we read. We write carefully and reverently as a means of staying longer with the text and exploring its implications. As we do it, the word is imprinted more fully on our consciousness and there is a greater possibility that it will continue to exercise an influence over us in the future." [2]

By writing, the Word becomes our own. The great American author Tobias Wolff a few years ago published a wonderful novel entitled *Old School*. It's about an exclusive boys' school where the students compete for the honor of a personal meeting with a visiting literary luminary. The competition takes the form of an original story-writing contest. The writer of the best story gets to have dinner

---

[2] Michael Casey, *Sacred Reading: The Ancient Art of LECTIO DIVINA* (Liguori: Triumph, 1995), p. 84.

with a world-renowned author. The main character of the novel wants very much to win, and he is doing everything he can to figure out how. He tells us:

> I'd read an article about a writer's colony in Marshall, Illinois, where the aspirants spent their mornings transcribing masterworks in order to learn what it actually felt like to write something great. James Jones had been associated with this group. If the practice helped him write *From Here to Eternity*, why couldn't it help me? ... None of this seemed ridiculous to me. A friend's parents back home had learned complicated dances by following footprints on diagrams they rolled out on the floor. I'd seen them do the mambo very impressively at a Christmas party.... They weren't even watching their feet. They were just doing what came naturally, from instincts they had trained with certain devotions, and the result was invention, freedom—mambo![3]

If you want to evangelize like an Evangelist, experience what it feels like literally to write like one. The result will be invention, freedom—preaching!

Don't wait to write. With your single sheet in front of you, start writing down your thoughts and impressions immediately. Mark, annotate, highlight, underline what you have transcribed. Work from this, your single sheet of paper now covered with Holy Writ, as you go about the task of actualizing the Scripture and as you consult theological dictionaries and other sources. Use the margins to inscribe possible points you may want to address ... questions that come to you ... problems to solve, etc. Write down anything that comes to mind. As Flannery O'Connor was reputed to say, "I write because I don't know what I think until I read what I say." The same holds true for preaching.

[3] Tobias Wolff, *Old School* (New York: Alfred A. Knopf, 2003), pp. 98–99.

William Zinsser, in his classic book *Writing to Learn*, says that "writing is thinking on paper.... Writing enables us to find out what we know—and what we don't know—about whatever we're trying to learn."[4]

About the writing process, John Henry Newman comments: "I think that writing is a stimulus to the mental faculties, to the logical talent, to originality, to the power of illustration, to the arrangement of topics, second to none. Till a man begins to put down his thought about a subject on paper he will not ascertain what he knows and what he does not know; and still less will he be able to express what he does know."[5]

Meditate on your findings. Approach the sacred text as if it were a person. Ask yourself questions like these: How is Christ offering me an encounter with his Presence in this Scripture passage? Concretely, how does this Scripture appeal to my need for beauty, truth, goodness, love, justice, happiness? In what way does this Word of God correspond with my heart? How does this text provoke me, change me? What is the lived question that this passage raises? What is the "problem" that it exposes—or that it *creates*—for my situation? How does it provide an answer to the ultimate questions of my life about suffering, meaning, direction, purpose? How does this passage reawaken the religious sense, and what response of faith does it provoke? How does this Scripture text raise an ultimate question in me, and what is the answer that it gives?

[4] William K. Zinsser, *Writing to Learn* (New York: HarperCollins, 1993), pp. ii, 16.

[5] John Henry Newman, *The Idea of a University* (Notre Dame: Notre Dame University Press, 1982), part 2, art. 6.6, p. 319.

All these queries return us to the level of our *I* where the Word of God desires to speak to us, addressing our elementary experience—our heart—and where Christ proposes himself as the totalizing Answer to our every question and need. Newman emphasizes that "it is the preacher's duty to aim at imparting to others ... some *definite* spiritual good.... The more exact and precise is the subject which he treats, the more impressive and practical will he be; whereas no one will carry off much from a discourse which is on the general subject of virtue, or vaguely and feebly entertains the question of the desirableness of attaining heaven, or the rashness of incurring eternal ruin." [6]

Summarize your homily in one short sentence. Edgar Allan Poe said that a story should be written for the sake of the last sentence. If the story is well conceived, composed, and told, then that last sentence will be a climax. It will effect great satisfaction in the hearer, making the story memorable and showing it to be sublime (as we discussed the notion in chapter 4). One culminating sentence determines the whole story. In a certain sense, the entire story is contained in that last sentence ... which is the first sentence that the writer conceives. The same is true in a way for preaching. A homily should be composed, not necessarily for the sake of the *last* sentence, but for the sake of one bottom-line, ultimate sentence that the preacher has firmly in mind as he approaches his preparation for preaching.

Once the hard work of *lectio divina* and actualization is done, the preacher must come up with *the one truest claim* that he can make as a result of his interaction with the

---

[6] Ibid., part 2, art. 6.3, p. 306.

sacred text. This claim is a *judgment*—the preacher's judgment, which he knows to be true because it is verified in
his own experience. The judgment is to be expressed in a
statement of no more than ten words. Then this précis of
the preacher's prayer becomes the sacrosanct core of his
entire homily preparation; it is the engine that drives everything. To quote again the Venerable J. H. Newman: "Nay,
I would go the length of recommending a preacher to place
a distinct categorical proposition before him, such as he can
write down in a form of words, and to guide and limit his
preparation by it, and to aim in all he says to bring it out,
and nothing else." [7]

By abiding by this self-imposed creative constraint, the
preacher's earnestness appears. As Newman explains,

> Nor will a preacher's earnestness show itself in anything
> more unequivocally than in his rejecting, whatever be the
> temptation to admit it, every remark, however original,
> every period, however eloquent, which does not in some
> way or other tend to bring out this one distinct propo-
> sition which he has chosen.... *Definiteness of object* is in
> various ways the one virtue of the preacher.... What he
> feels himself, and feels deeply, he has to make others feel
> deeply; and in proportion as he comprehends this, he will
> rise above the temptation of introducing collateral mat-
> ters, and will have not taste, no heart for going aside after
> flowers of oratory, fine figures, tuneful periods, which are
> worth nothing, unless they come to him spontaneously,
> and are spoken "out of the abundance of the heart.". . .
> Definiteness is the life of preaching. [8]

This summarizing statement is to be put in the form of
a *proposal*, that is, a claim that engages the hearers' freedom,

[7] Ibid.
[8] Ibid.

prompting them to make a judgment ... *and* that hope-
fully moves them to assent. Von Balthasar counsels us not
to presuppose the faith but rather to propose it. Faith is not
a "finished business" that we can simply take for granted;
the life of faith has to be constantly renewed.

Use compelling examples. The way that people will be certain that what a preacher proposes to them is true is through
well-chosen examples that verify the preacher's claim. They
"flesh it out". In fact, if you cannot present compelling
examples, illustrations, applications, images, or analogies to
verify your claim, then your hearers will conclude that what
you are telling them is either not true or not important ...
because it remains an abstraction—and *no one wants to follow an abstraction*. It insults our humanity, which is hard-
wired to find the Infinite by way of the finite.

Well-selected examples are indispensable to authentic
Gospel preaching because they substantiate a preacher's
claim by showing how a concrete Word becomes flesh here
and now. Examples honor our need to know from the starting point of our experience. An excellent example is so
precisely because of the exquisite *correspondence* that it sets
up between a Word proposed and the reality of the hearer's life. Then, a connection that I never saw before I suddenly see, and it excites me, enthralls me. I understand.
Now it's clear. And I'm never going to forget it.

Realistically, the examples a preacher uses are usually
what people remember most about preaching. This *attests
to just how human a thing examples are!* Obviously, examples
are the way we think about, organize, and make sense of
reality. Examples are the way we remember it.

But good examples are hard to find. That is why a major
part of your homily preparation will consist not so much

in studying sources or composing thoughts as in *being attentive to reality*. Once you have the central conviction about
what you want to preach, then your mind becomes like a
magnet drawn to things in the news, in conversations, in
the arts, in your reading, your ministry, your recreation,
your memory, and your ordinary dealings with others that
verify your homiletic position and that offer themselves as
good illustrations for what you plan to say.

But this process cannot be forced or rushed. This is why
a preacher must build time into his preaching preparation
schedule that gives him the luxury to be attentive to whatever may come his way to help him preach persuasively. I
have a priest friend who spends time during his summer
vacation outlining his Sunday homilies for the coming fall
as he casually reads different newspapers, magazines, and the
novels and other books that he has saved up for his time off.
He does this in a relaxed, no-pressure kind of way (that I
think he actually enjoys) ... and his homiletic results are
spectacular all because he attunes the radar for great stories early. The reality is that if a preacher does not ascertain early in the week what he plans to preach on Sunday,
the chance for such rich assimilation is squandered.

Determine the length of your homily according to a proper
proportionality. Personally, I'm in favor of shorter homilies. I think eight minutes is an ideal length for a Sunday
homily because you can actually *say something* in eight minutes. And if a preacher *can't* manage to get a worthwhile
point across in eight minutes, chances are slim that he will
pull it off in ten minutes or twelve (the longer the homily
goes, the more the attention span wanes). But the eight-
minute guideline also ensures that the proper proportionality of the Mass is respected: the homily will not be longer

than the most important element of the Liturgy, the Eucharistic Prayer.

What about form or structure? My recommendation for this is to keep it very simple. You have your one, summarizing sentence that gives focus to your whole homily. That statement is a proposal. That *is* your homily. So, introduce it briefly (one minute). State it (one minute). Help people to see why it is crucial for their lives (two minutes). Give an example to illustrate what you meant (one minute). Give another example (one minute). Apply your proposal to the people's lives concretely, that is, the action they are to take (one minute); give your ending (one minute).

Preach without a manuscript. Perhaps one of the most terrifying facets of preaching is the idea of preaching without having a text with you in the pulpit (or not being in the pulpit at all!). Apart from this being the most ancient mode of preaching, it is also the most logical since the point of preaching is to regenerate others. How can a genuine encounter happen if you are "on book"? Preaching without a script in front of you ensures immediacy, contact, engagement, rapport. Would you ever go to see a play in which the actors had not memorized the script? No—you would demand your money back. How can you interact with the artistry of the actor and the playwright if the play has not been learned by heart? Have you ever heard of a father who reared his child while holding a parenting manual in hand? We would judge that absurd; we would think there was something seriously wrong with the man and doubt his competency as a father. The same holds for preaching, for preaching is regenerating.

The preacher's great "fear" of preaching without a text is that he will forget something. But the reality is that if the preacher's proposal has not been personally appropriated to the point that the preacher is able to deliver a homily without the assistance of printed aids, then in fact he is not really preaching from his experience; he is preaching ideas (worthy and true as they may be). When we become what we preach, a text is superfluous.

Preaching without a text is duly terrifying because it means putting ourselves on the line; it means taking a big risk. But nothing moves and compels people like a man of conviction speaking his convictions ... no matter how many infinitives he splits, modifiers he misplaces, or participles he dangles.

And *so what* if we get lost, lose our place, or forget a point when preaching without a text? The display of a preacher's humanity and vulnerability in front of his people will only make them love the preacher more and *listen more attentively*. I know of one (naughty) preacher who used to *pretend* to get lost precisely to provoke this response in his congregation (not recommended).

At one point in my life, I had the great honor of helping out on Sundays at a parish in Yonkers, New York. The pastor was a holy, prayerful priest who was full of love (he died of cancer at a young age). One weekend he presupposed that he had assigned me to celebrate the Saturday evening vigil Mass, ... but he hadn't. And he did not discover this oversight until just a few minutes before the Mass was scheduled to begin. This priest was in the habit of writing out his Sunday homily word for word and reading it from the pulpit. But he had not yet finished his draft of his homily for that Sunday. Yet, with the mix-up, he was the only priest available to celebrate the vigil Mass. So, for the first time in who knows how long, he preached without a text. And scads of people went up to him afterward to tell him how great his preaching was. They loved it!

Siding with me in this is someone of no less authority than John Henry Cardinal Newman:

> In truth, a discourse, which, from its fineness and precision of ideas, is too difficult for a preacher to deliver without such extraneous assistance, is too difficult for a hearer to follow; and, if a book be imperative for teaching, it is imperative for learning.... Preaching is not reading, and reading is not preaching.... For myself, I think it no extravagance to say that a very inferior sermon, delivered without book, answers the purposes for which all sermons are delivered more perfectly than one of great merit, if it be written and read.[9]

In fact, if a preacher insists on preparing a verbatim text that includes every single word of a homily that he intends to preach, then Newman directs that "both parties ought to read, if they are to be on equal terms". That is, the printed homily should be distributed to the congregation so that they can read along. And this arrangement makes perfect sense, for I can get considerably more out of printed text if I have the chance to study the words on the page. Then I can go at my own pace; I can reread any sections that aren't quite clear to me or that I would like to reinforce in my memory. Also, it is altogether likely that certain members of the congregation may be better readers of a printed page than we preachers are speakers of it.

However, *always* be sure to *memorize your ending*. You must be absolutely certain about how you intend to conclude your homily. Remember: if a pilot is not sure how

[9] Ibid., part 2, art. 6.6, 7.

to land the plane, he is not the only person onboard who is nervous.

Speak directly to the people. Your time in the pulpit is shorter than you think. Get right to it. Eschew formalism, artifice, affectation. Speak to your people personally, directly, not beating around the bush, in a conversational tone, from your heart like a father with something important to tell his children. Preaching is an encounter—especially in its delivery. Preaching is meant to offer people a presence that rescues them from the powerlessness of solitude and isolation. It is the offering, not of an idea or a message, but of *something that is happening* through *someone.* Thus, the *way* that the preacher speaks is instrumental to bringing this happening about. As Newman notes in the epigraph to the chapter, "People are drawn and moved, not simply by what is said, but by how it is said, and who says it." [10]

With good intentions, we preachers want to be *earnest* in our preachment. And earnestness is excellent, for, as Newman explains, "earnestness creates earnestness in others by sympathy; and the more a preacher loses and is lost to himself, the more does he gain his brethren.... For what is powerful enough to absorb and possess a preacher has at least a *prima facie* claim of attention on the part of his hearers. On the other hand, anything which interferes with this earnestness, or which argues its absence, is still more certain to blunt the force of the most cogent argument conveyed in the most eloquent language." [11] Therefore, the best way to attain earnestness in preaching is that of self-forgetfulness. The surest means to effecting earnestness is

[10] Ibid., part 2, art. 6.6.
[11] Ibid., part 2, art. 6.2, p. 305.

allowing ourselves to be absorbed and possessed by our encounter with Christ.

Newman is even more insistent: "I do not mean that a preacher must aim at *earnestness*, but that he must aim at his *object*. . . . To sit down to compose for the pulpit with a resolution to be eloquent is one impediment to persuasion; but to be determined to be earnest is absolutely fatal to it." [12] To support his point, Newman offers this superb analogy: "It is said that, when a man has to cross an abyss by a narrow plank thrown over it, it is his wisdom not to look at the plank along which lies his path, but to fix his eyes steadily on the point in the opposite precipice at which the plank ends. It is by gazing at the object which he must reach, and ruling himself by it, that he secures to himself the power of walking to it straight and steadily." [13]

Don't try this at home: Not long ago it was my turn to preach at a community Mass in a Dominican priory. The congregation consisted of venerable older friars, a few priests who were my peers, not to mention a number of zealous student brothers preparing for the priesthood—all in all, a lethal combination. (There's no more daunting an audience to preach to than to "our own".) I had something definite to propose all right, . . . but I let myself get intimidated by the potentially hypercritical evaluation to which I was exposing myself. And rather than becoming "lost to myself" and "absorbed and possessed by my proposal", I let myself obsess about whether I "would make a good impression", etc. And so I preached, . . . but clearly something was off. One of the concelebrants was my friend Father Jacek Buda, O.P., an incontrovertible critic. He told

12 Ibid., part 2, art. 6.3, p. 306.
13 Ibid.

me: "It was good. What you had to say was something. But something was missing. This was not really *yourself*." And he was right! I was "aiming at earnestness" . . . and that is fatal. But it didn't get by him.

Father Buda said to me, "When you preach, just *tell us!*" And this is the point. A preacher may be duly proud of his scintillating syntax. But in the end it's not going to matter much because people are not going to remember it. Rather, they will remember *what happened*. Speaking directly and personally to people when we preach ensures that preaching is a *happening* . . . that is, an event. And *that* is unforgettable.

Preaching Why

"God I worship in the spirit by preaching the Gospel of his Son"

—SAINT PAUL (Rom 1:9, NAB)

THE AIM OF PREACHING, as Pope Benedict XVI has told us, "is to tell man who he is and what he must do to be himself. Its intention is to disclose to him the truth about himself, that is, what he can base his life on and what he can die for."[1] We preach to bring about the reconquest of humanity. People need a reason to leave behind the countless compromises and concessions that they have settled for in their lives. People need a reason to dare to believe; they need a reason to endeavor to trust. People need to know why it is reasonable to come out from the darkness instead of staying secluded in it . . . to let down the walls that seem to protect but that end up only alienating. People need to know why it is reasonable to expect in their lives Something More. That is, people need a reason—an irrefutable reason—to live their life as *a risk*.

Good preaching is preaching filled with that reason (see 1 Pet 3:15). Good preaching is good precisely because it

[1] Joseph Cardinal Ratzinger, *The Nature and Mission of Theology*, trans. Adrian Walker (San Francisco: Ignatius Press, 1995), p. 62.

tells people who they are; it gives them back the humanity they had long forgotten, immersed as they are in the
oblivion of spiritual amnesia. To preach well is to preach
why the proposal of the Gospel makes infinitely more sense
than any of the mentalities, preconceptions, or ideologies
that vie to brainwash people. To preach well is to preach
why Jesus Christ makes all the difference in our life. To
preach well is to preach the supreme reasonableness of saying Yes to Christ's offer of self—to the encounter. To preach
well is to preach why it is right to hope.

As Father Julián Carrón tells us, that hope does not come
from what we do, but from the awareness that there is
Someone who loves us with an everlasting love, who calls
us into being every instant, having pity on our nothing-
ness. The priest as preacher becomes this alter-Someone
whose paternal love fills others with hope. Because of his
witness we know why we should heed his preaching . . .
why his preaching is the Answer for me.

Good preaching is preaching filled with reasons that
make people eager to live their humanity, their *I*, again.
Why should I believe a preacher's preaching? Because the
preacher who preaches the Gospel speaks of happiness . . .
and whenever we speak of happiness we become attractive
to others. To preach well is to preach why no one should
give up on happiness.

If every day of our lives we live regenerated by the
encounter with Christ, then we have all we need to preach
why and to preach well. Lacordaire says, "You have everything necessary in preaching God's word with fruit—strong
faith, genuine piety, true disinterestedness, a wish to make
God known and loved, and lastly, natural gifts quite sufficient to support those of grace. Work hard, and the tal-
ents put into your charge will increase in proportion to

the pains you take. No degree of fluency will avail without work: that is the key to eloquence and to knowledge, as well as to virtue." [2]

Jesus Christ himself has prayed for us and for those who will come to believe because of our word (see Jn 17:20). This gives us every reason to approach our preaching with confident and daring boldness. Monsignor Lorenzo Albacete tells the story of a Father Nembrini—a missionary priest who was sent alone to bring the Gospel to the people in a remote village of Kazakhstan. The villagers had never heard of Jesus Christ; they had been brought up in the strictures of Marxist Communism. He needed to teach them about the Resurrection. What could he ever say to get them to understand the meaning of the Resurrection and to move them to believe? He told them the only thing that was possible—he said to them, "Look at me; stay with me." And the more the people observed Father Nembrini's life and what made him different, that is, happy, peaceful, certain, self-sacrificing, etc., the more they concluded that there had to be a reason for the priest's exceptionality. And that Exceptionality, which they discovered in the flesh of another person whom they had encountered, they began to call "Christ".

The fourteenth-century Eastern theologian Nicholas Cabasilas made the observation that when those who have in them a desire so powerful that it surpasses their nature, then Christ sends a burning ray of his beauty into their eyes that lets other people intuit who Christ is. When we look into the eyes of a preacher in love with Jesus Christ, that is enough for us. That is the reason why to believe, to follow,

[2] Henri-Dominique Lacordaire, *Letter XLVI: "Advice to a Young Priest"* in *Letters to Young Men*, trans. James Trenor (London: Art and Book Co., 1902), p. 95.

to live life as a risk, as an obedience of joy. It all comes down to the beauty of the preacher. Pope John Paul II said it best: "Beauty makes one feel the beginning of ... ful-fillment, and seems to whisper to us: 'You will not be unhappy; the desire of your heart will be fulfilled, what is more, it is already being fulfilled.' " [3] Fulfilled in their hear-ing of your preaching.

---

[3] John Paul II, *Message to the Participants in the 23rd Meeting for Friendship among Peoples Held in Rimini* (August 19, 2002).

BIBLIOGRAPHY OF WORKS CITED
OR CONSULTED

Alberto, Stefano. "The 'I' and the Revolution of the Faith". *Traces* 8, no. 3 (2006): 51–52.

Alonso Schökel, Luis. *The Inspired Word: Scripture in the Light of Language and Literature.* New York: Herder and Herder, 1965.

———. *A Manual of Hermeneutics.* Sheffield: Sheffield Academic Press, 1998.

Aquinas, Thomas. *Contra Impugnantes Dei Cultum et Religionem.*

———. *In Isaias.*

———. *In Jeremiam.*

———. *In Matt.*

———. *Summa Contra Gentiles.*

Augustine of Hippo. *Confessions.* Trans. R. S. Pine-Coffin. New York: Penguin, 1961.

———. *Contra Iulianum opus imperfectum.*

———. *On Christian Doctrine.* Upper Saddle River: Library of Liberal Arts, 1958.

Baldwin, James. *Blues for Mister Charlie.* New York: Laurel/Dell, 1964.

Balthasar, Hans Urs von. *Seeing the Form.* Vol. 1 of *The Glory of the Lord.* San Francisco: Ignatius Press, 1982.

———. *The Grain of Wheat: Aphorisms.* San Francisco: Ignatius Press, 1995.

———. *Love Alone Is Credible.* San Francisco: Ignatius Press, 2005.

———. *The Word Made Flesh.* Vol. 1 of *Explorations in Theology.* San Francisco: Ignatius Press, 1989.

Bauer, Walter, and Frederick William Danker, eds. *A Greek-English Lexicon of the New Testament and Other Early Christian Literature*. Chicago: University of Chicago Press, 2000.

Benedict XVI (Joseph Ratzinger). "I Send You Out on the Great Mission of Evangelizing", Address to Youth. Pacaembu, Brazil. May 10, 2007.

———. "Address to the Participants at the Ecclesial Convention of the Diocese of Rome". June 5, 2006.

———. "Cardinal Ratzinger Tells Why Many Misperceive Christianity" (May 7, 2004): http://www.zenit.org/article-10033?l=english.

———. *Co-Workers of the Truth*. San Francisco: Ignatius Press, 1992.

———. *The Feast of Faith: Approaches to a Theology of the Liturgy*. San Francisco: Ignatius Press, 1986.

———. "The Feeling of Things, the Contemplation of Beauty". Message to the Communion and Liberation Meeting at Rimini, Italy (August 2002). Published as "Cardinal Ratzinger on the Contemplation of Beauty". *Zenit* (May 2, 2005): http://www.zenit.org/article-12907?l=english.

———. *God Is Love. Deus Caritas Est*. San Francisco: Ignatius Press, 2006.

———. *Gospel, Catechesis, Catechism: Sidelights on the "Catechism of the Catholic Church"*. San Francisco: Ignatius Press, 1997.

———. *Introduction to Christianity*. Trans. J.R. Foster. 2nd ed. San Francisco: Ignatius Press, 2004.

———. *Jesus of Nazareth*. San Francisco: Ignatius Press, 2008.

———. *The Nature and Mission of Theology*. Trans. Adrian Walker. San Francisco: Ignatius Press, 1995.

———. "The Power and the Grace". In *30 Days*, no. 10 (1998): 31–32.

———. *Principles of Catholic Theology*. Trans. Sr. Mary Frances McCarthy. San Francisco: Ignatius Press, 1987.

————. *Sacramentum Caritatis*. 2007.

————. *Truth and Tolerance: Christian Belief and World Religions*. Trans. Henry Taylor. San Francisco: Ignatius Press, 2004.

————. *A Turning Point for Europe?* Trans. Brian McNeil, C.R.V. San Francisco: Ignatius Press, 1994.

Berlioz, Hector. *The Memoirs of Hector Berlioz*. Trans. David Cairns. New York: Alfred A. Knopf, 1969.

Bouyer, Louis. *Introduction to Spirituality*. New York: Desclée, 1961.

Cabasilas, Nicholas. *The Life in Christ*. Crestwood: St. Vladimir's Seminary Press, 1998.

Caffarra, Carlo. Quoted in Andrea Tornielli, "Inversion of Method". *Traces* 4, no. 1 (2002): 30–31.

Cameron, Peter John. "The Catechism on Preaching". *Crisis* 14, no. 6 (June 1996): 39–43.

————. "Is It Really Good News?" *America* 175, no. 2 (July 20–27, 1996): 21–22.

————. *To Praise, To Bless, To Preach—Cycle A*. Huntington, Ind.: Our Sunday Visitor, 2000.

————. *To Praise, To Bless, To Preach—Cycle B*. Huntington, Ind.: Our Sunday Visitor, 1999.

————. *To Praise, To Bless, To Preach—Cycle C*. Huntington, Ind.: Our Sunday Visitor, 2001.

Camisasca, Massimo. *Fraternity and Mission* (Newsletter). Rome, Italy, June 2003.

Campbell, Joseph. *The Power of Myth*. New York: Anchor, 1991.

Cantalamessa, Raniero. *Life in Christ: A Spiritual Commentary on the Letter to the Romans*. Collegeville, Minn.: The Liturgical Press, 2002.

————. *The Mystery of God's Word*. Collegeville, Minn.: The Liturgical Press, 1994.

————. *The Mystery of Pentecost*. Collegeville, Minn.: The Liturgical Press, 2001.

Casey, Michael. *Sacred Reading: The Ancient Art of* Lectio Div-
    ina. Liguori: Triumph, 1995.

Catechism of the Catholic Church. Second ed. Vatican City: Libre-
    ria Editrice Vaticana, 1997.

Cessario, Romanus. *Introduction to Moral Theology.* Washington,
    D.C.: The Catholic University of America Press, 2001.

—— et al. *The Love That Never Ends: A Key to the Catechism
    of the Catholic Church.* Huntington, Ind.: Our Sunday Visitor
    Press, 1996.

Code of Canon Law.

Communion and Liberation. *Event of Freedom: Exercises of the Fra-
    ternity of Communion and Liberation.* Rimini, 2003.

——. *The Miracle of a Change: Exercises of the Fraternity of Com-
    munion and Liberation.* Rimini, 1998.

——. *Origin and Power of the "I": International Assembly of Com-
    munion and Liberation Responsibles.* Milan: Traces, 1999.

——. *You Live for Love of Something Happening Now: Exercises of
    Fraternity of Communion and Liberation.* Rimini, 2006.

——. *You or About Friendship: Exercises of the Fraternity of Com-
    munion and Liberation.* Rimini, 1997.

Congar, Yves. "Sacramental Worship and Preaching". In *The
    Renewal of Preaching: Theory and Practice.* Vol. 33 of *Concilium.*
    New York: Paulist Press, 1968.

Congregation for the Clergy. *The Priest and the Third Christian
    Millennium, Teacher of the Word, Minister of the Sacraments, and
    Leader of the Community.* 1999.

——. *The Priest, Pastor and Leader of the Parish Community.* 2002.

Daniélou, Jean. *Christ and Us.* Trans. Walter Roberts. New York:
    Sheed and Ward, 1961.

Darton, Michael. *Modern Concordance to the New Testament.* Gar-
    den City: Doubleday, 1976.

De Montfort, Louis Marie. *God Alone: The Collected Writings of
    St. Louis Marie De Montfort.* Bayshore, N.Y.: Montfort Publi-
    cations, 1995.

Fallows, James. "Reading by Ear". In *The Atlantic Monthly* 287, no. 1 (2001): 16–17.

General Instruction to the Roman Missal. 3rd typical ed. 2002.

Giussani, Luigi. *At the Origin of the Christian Claim*. Montreal: McGill-Queen's University Press, 1998.

———. "Recognizing Christ: The First Accents of a New Morality". In *Communion and Liberation: A Movement in the Church*. Edited by David Rondoni. Translated by Patrick Stevenson and Susan Scott. Montreal: McGill-Queens, 2000.

———. *The Religious Sense*. Montreal: McGill-Queen's University Press, 1997.

———. *The Risk of Education*. New York: Crossroad, 2001.

———. *Why the Church?* Montreal: McGill-Queen's University Press, 2001.

Hadler, Susan J., and Ann Bennett Mix. *Lost in the Victory: Reflections of American War Orphans of World War II*. Ed. Calvin L. Christman. Denton: University of North Texas Press, 1998.

Hahn, Scott. *A Father Who Keeps His Promises*. Cincinnati: Servant Publications, 1998.

Herbert, Zbigniew. *The Collected Poems, 1956–1998*. Trans. Alissa Valles. New York: HarperCollins Publishers, 2007.

Hill, William J. "What Is Preaching? One Heuristic Model from Theology". In *A New Look at Preaching*, ed. John Burke. Wilmington: Michael Glazier, 1983.

Humbert of Romans. *A Treatise on Preaching*. Westminster: Newman Press, 1951.

John of the Cross. *The Collected Works of St. John of the Cross*. Washington, D.C.: ICS Publications, 1979.

John Paul II (Karol Wojtyła). "Address to the Participants in the Third 'Meeting for Friendship between Peoples'". Rimini, August 29, 1982.

———. *Celebration of the Word at Mount Sinai*. February 26, 2000.

———. *Crossing the Threshold of Hope*. New York: Knopf, 1995.

———. *Fides et Ratio*. 1998.

————. *Gift and Mystery*. New York: Image Books, 1996.

————. "Letter to Msgr. Luigi Giussani". February 11, 2002.

————. "Letter to Msgr. Luigi Giussani on the Occasion of the 50th Anniversary of the Movement 'Communion and Liberation'". February 22, 2004.

————. *Love and Responsibility*. New York: Farrar, Straus and Giroux, 1981.

————. "Message of His Holiness John Paul II, signed by the Secretary of State, Cardinal Angelo Sodano, to the Participants in the 23rd Meeting for Friendship among Peoples Held in Rimini". August 19, 2002.

————. *Pastores Dabo Vobis*. 1992.

————. *The Radiation of Fatherhood*. In *The Collected Plays and Writings on Theater by Pope John Paul II*. Trans. Boleslaw Taborski. Berkeley: University of California Press, 1987.

————. *Salvifici Doloris*. 1984.

Keller, Helen. *The Story of My Life*. New York: Bantam, 1990.

Lacordaire, Henri-Dominique. *Letters to Young Men*. London: Art and Book Co., 1902.

Lavelle, Louis. *The Dilemma of Narcissus*. Burdett: Larson Publications, 1993.

————. *Evil and Suffering*. Trans. Bernard Murchland. New York: The Macmillan Co., 1963.

Lewis, C. S. *The Problem of Pain*. San Francisco: HarperCollins, 1996.

Lineamenta of the Synod on the Word of God.

Longinus. *On the Sublime*.

Magrassi, Mariano. *Praying the Bible: An Introduction to* Lectio Divina. Collegeville, Minn.: The Liturgical Press, 1998.

Maritain, Raïssa. *Raïssa's Journal*. Albany: Magi, 1974.

Martin, Francis. *Encounter Story: A Characteristic Gospel Narrative Form*. Washington, D.C.: Mother of God Services, 1979.

————. *Sacred Scripture: The Disclosure of the Word*. Naples: Sapientia Press, 2006.

National Conference of Catholic Bishops. *Fulfilled in Your Hearing: The Homily in the Sunday Assembly*. Washington, D.C.: U.S. Catholic Conference, 1982.

Newman, John Henry. *The Idea of a University*. Notre Dame: University of Notre Dame Press, 1982.

Ong, Walter J. *The Presence of the Word: Some Prolegomena for Cultural and Religious History*. New Haven: Yale University Press, 1967.

Pascal, Blaise. *Pensées*. Trans. W. F. Trotter. New York: E.P. Dutton and Co., 1958.

Pieper, Josef. *Faith, Hope, Love*. Trans. Richard and Clara Winston and Sr. Mary Frances McCarthy. San Francisco: Ignatius Press, 1997.

Pinckaers, Servais. *Morality: The Catholic View*. South Bend, Ind.: St. Augustine's Press, 2001.

Pontifical Biblical Commission. *The Interpretation of the Bible in the Church*. 1993.

Powell, Mark Allan. *What Is Narrative Criticism?* Minneapolis: Fortress Press, 1990.

Rock, Augustine. *Unless They Be Sent: A Theological Study of the Nature and Purpose of Preaching*. London: Blackfriars Publications, 1955.

Rondoni, Davide. *Communion and Liberation: A Movement in the Church*. Translated by Patrick Stevenson and Susan Scott. Montreal: McGill-Queens, 2000.

Rover, Dominic. "Preaching, III (Theology of)". *New Catholic Encyclopedia*. Vol. 11. Washington, D.C.: The Catholic University of America Press, 1967.

The Rule of St. Benedict.

Sertillanges, Antonin. *Spirituality*. New York: McMullen Books, 1954.

Sokolowski, Robert. *The God of Faith and Reason: Foundation of Christian Theology*. Washington, D.C.: The Catholic University Press, 1995.

Vanier, Jean. *Be Not Afraid*. Ramsey: Paulist Press, 1975.

———. *Followers of Jesus*. Guelph: Alive Press Ltd., 1973.

Vann, Gerald. *The Divine Pity: A Study in the Social Implications of the Beatitudes*. New York: Scepter, 2007.

Vatican Council II. Dogmatic Constitution on Divine Revelation *Dei Verbum*. 1965.

———. Pastoral Constitution on the Church in the Modern World *Gaudium et Spes*. 1965.

Vincent Ferrer, St. *A Treatise on the Spiritual Life*. Washington, D.C.: Dominicana, 1957.

The Way of the Pilgrim. Trans. Helen Bacovcin. Garden City: Doubleday Image, 1978.

Wilbur, Richard. *Mayflies: New Poems and Translations*. New York: Houghton Mifflin Harcourt Publishing, 2000.

Wilder, Amos N. *Early Christian Rhetoric: The Language of the Gospel*. Cambridge: Harvard University Press, 1971.

Wojtyła, Karol. *The Collected Plays and Writings on Theater*. Trans. Boleslaw Taborski. Berkeley: University of California Press, 1987.

———. *Love and Responsibility*. Trans. H. T. Willetts. San Francisco: Ignatius Press, 1993.

Wolff, Tobias. *Old School*. New York: Alfred A. Knopf, 2003.

Zinsser, William K. *Writing to Learn*. New York: HarperCollins, 1993.

Zundel, Maurice. *The Gospel Within*. Sherbrooke: Editions Paulines, 1993.

———. *The Inner Person, Finding God Within*, Sherbrooke: Médiaspaul, 1996.

ACKNOWLEDGMENTS

The author is deeply grateful to the publishers and copyright holders listed below for their kind permission to reprint in this book material from the following sources:

At the Origin of the Christian Claim by Luigi Giussani. Translated by Viviane Hewitt. Montreal: McGill-Queen's University Press, © 1998. Used by permission.

Be Not Afraid by Jean Vanier. Ramsay: Paulist Press, © 1975 Jean Vanier. Used by permission.

Communion and Liberation: A Movement in the Church. Edited by Davide Rondoni. Translated by Patrick Stevenson and Susan Scott. Montreal: McGill-Queen's University Press, © 2000. Used by permission.

Confessions by Saint Augustine, translated with an introduction by R. S. Pine-Coffin (Penguin Classics, 1961). Copyright © R. S. Pine-Coffin, 1961. London: Penguin Books Limited. Reproduced by permission of Penguin Books Limited.

The Dilemma of Narcissus by Louis Lavelle. Translated by W. T. Gairdner. Burdett: Larson Publications, © 1993. Used by permission.

The Divine Pity: A Study in the Social Implications of the Beatitudes by Rev. Gerald Vann, O.P. New York: Scepter, © 2007. Used by permission.

Early Christian Rhetoric: The Language of the Gospel by Amos N. Wilder. Pp. 12–13, 48, 54, 57, 60, 68, 84. Cambridge, Mass.: Harvard University Press, Copyright © 1971

Excerpt from "A Barred Owl" in *Mayflies: New Poems and Translations*, copyright © 2000 by Richard Wilbur, reprinted by permission of Houghton Mifflin Harcourt Publishing Company.

Morality: The Catholic View by Servais Pinckaers, O.P. Translated by Michael Sherwin, O.P. South Bend: St. Augustine's Press, © 2001. Used by permission.

The Mystery of Pentecost by Raniero Cantalamessa, O.F.M. Cap. Translated by Glen S. Davis. Collegeville: The Liturgical Press, © 2001. Used by permission.

The Mystery of God's Word by Raniero Cantalamessa. Translated by Alan Neame. Collegeville: The Liturgical Press, © 1994. Used by permission.

From *Old School* by Tobias Wolff, copyright © 2003 by Tobias Wolff. Used by permission of Alfred A. Knopf, a division of Random House, Inc.

Praying the Bible: An Introduction to Lectio Divina by Mariano Magrassi, O.S.B. Translated by Edward Hagman, O.F.M. Cap. Collegeville: Liturgical Press, © 1998. Used by permission.

The Presence of the Word: Some Prolegomena for Cultural and Religious History by Walter J. Ong, S.J. New Haven: Yale University Press, © 1967. Used by permission.

Excerpt from "Reading By Ear" by James Fallows, *The Atlantic Monthly*, January, 2001. Copyright 2001 The Atlantic Monthly Group, as first published in *The Atlantic Monthly*.

The Religious Sense by Luigi Giussani. Translated by John Zucchi. Montreal: McGill-Queen's University Press, 1997. © 1997. Used by permission.

The Risk of Education: Discovering Our Ultimate Destiny by Luigi Giussani. Translated by Rosanna M. Giammanco

INDEX